# SIMPLY SLIM

## THE TOTALLY HEALTHY
## VEGETARIAN DIET PLAN

GW00482839

# SIMPLY SLIM

## THE TOTALLY HEALTHY VEGETARIAN DIET PLAN

## Margaret Cousins

*Illustrated by Juliet Breese*

THORSONS PUBLISHING GROUP
Wellingborough, Northamptonshire
Rochester, Vermont

First published 1987

British Library Cataloguing in Publication Data

Cousins, Margaret, *1949-*
Simply slim: the totally healthy vegetarian diet plan.
1. Reducing diets — Recipes     2. Vegetarian cookery
I. Title
641.5'636          RM222.2

ISBN 0-7225-1399-2


Printed and bound in Great Britain

1  3  5  7  9  10  8  6  4  2

# CONTENTS

I would like to express my appreciation to The Winston Churchill Memorial Trust whose travelling fellowship to the Middle East provided me with many ideas for this book as well as the determination to complete it.

# INTRODUCTION

## What Is This Book About?

It is a wholefood, daily diet guide that is vegetarian, balanced nutritionally and follows the latest recommendations for healthier eating. The calories are also counted so that you can assess the amount of food and drink you can consume to help you reach and/or maintain an optimum body-weight.

## Who Can Benefit From It?

Vegetarians who are interested in a balanced diet whether or not they are weightwatching/reducing.

Non vegetarians who are trying to reduce/exclude meat and fish from their diet and want to ensure that it still contains sufficient nutrients.

Non vegetarians who are weightwatching and realize the benefits of a vegetarian diet for slimmers.

## How Is It Useful?

This book emphasizes the need to choose from a wide range of fruit and vegetables (including whole grains, pulses, nuts and seeds) to achieve a diet that is adequate in terms of its protein, carbohydrate, fat, vitamin, mineral and fibre content.

● Using vegetable sources and lower fat dairy produce, sufficient protein of good quality is provided in the daily diet, even when the lowest calorie intake total is being followed.

● The total fat intake is reduced, especially in animal fats.

● Unrefined carbohydrate foods, which provide more nutrients and dietary fibre than the refined carbohydrates, form a significant part of the calorie total.

● This is a calorie intake guide that can be used whatever your age, sex, weight or lifestyle.

● It allows for flexibility and variety in the diet, providing a wide choice and the opportunity to use your own initiative.

● It can be used/adapted to incorporate other members of the family so that they can all benefit from an improved diet.

*Note*: If you have a known medical condition, you should consult your doctor before following this or any other food plan, in an attempt to lose weight.

# CUT — THE KEY WORD

Count The Calories
Up The Natural Fibre Foods
Trim The Fatty Foods

## Count The Calories

Calories are a measure of energy and, although our body needs energy in the form of food, people's energy requirements vary enormously. Two people of the same age, sex and height may have very different energy needs, depending on, for example, their lifestyles and how active they are. Consequently the level of food intake at which they gain weight will vary.

If your body is consistently taking in more calories than it is using to carry out its daily activities, then you are likely to put on weight. Calorie intake must be equal to the amount of energy your body is using if you are to maintain a steady weight. To lose weight you need to be taking in fewer calories than you are using. If you are overweight then it is just as important to exercise more as it is to count the calories.

If your weight is steady and you want to maintain this, it is worthwhile calculating your average daily intake and ensuring that it does not creep up, especially if you become less active.

If you are overweight assess your daily calorie intake and reduce it by a third or a half depending on weight loss required.

## Up The Natural Fibre Foods

Sugar, white flour and rice and their products are refined foods that have had some beneficial nutrients and much of the fibre removed during processing. Refined foods contribute calories, yet their poorer quality and insufficient bulk fails to satisfy hunger, which is bad news for slimmers!

These can be replaced by unrefined foods — fresh fruit and vegetables, whole grains (such as brown rice), peas, beans and lentils, nuts and seeds that, in a varied diet, will provide the necessary nutrients and the fibre needed to aid digestion. Such bulky foods also help to combat hunger.

## Trim The Fatty Foods

All major dietary guidelines are recommending a reduction in our total fat consumption. Fats have over twice as many calories as either protein or carbohydrate, and some, in excess, may be harmful to your body. There is also the suggestion that fats from plant sources may be preferable to those from animals.

This book therefore aims to reduce the total fat intake using only low or medium fat dairy produce, low fat spreads and, where necessary, vegetable fats and oils.

# THE FOOD PLAN

## Following The Plan

### Essentials

Each day ONE selection must be made from each of the following sections of this plan to ensure a nutritionally balanced diet. (Two selections can be made from either section 3 or 4 however, without upsetting the balance).

| | | |
|---|---|---|
| 1. Daily Allowance (of milk/yogurt + fat + fruit) (page 13) | providing 250 cals approx. | |
| 2. Breakfast (pages 14-19) | providing 150/200/300 cals approx. | |
| 3. Light/Easy Meals (pages 20-31) | providing 250/300/400/500 cals approx. | |
| 4. More Effort/Family Meals (pages 32-35) | providing 250/300/400/500 cals approx. | |
| 5. Desserts (pages 36-43) | providing 100/150/200/250 cals approx. | |

Whilst the minimum daily intake in this plan is therefore 1,000 cals approximately, there is no upper limit. Meals can always be combined or doubled in quantity and extras can easily be included (see Optional Extras below)

At least two vegetable portions (preferably fresh, with one as a salad) should be eaten daily. You will find that several of the meals in the Recipes section have an accompanying vegetable dish.

### 'Free' Vegetables

You can include the following vegetables in your diet in moderate quantities without worrying too much about their calorie content:

Artichokes, asparagus, aubergines, bamboo shoots, bean shoots, beetroot, broccoli, Brussels sprouts, cabbage, carrots, cauliflower, celeriac, celery, chickory, courgettes, cucumber, endive, green beans, leeks, lettuce, marrow, mushrooms, okra, onions, parsnips, green peas, pumpkin, radishes, spinach, swede, tomatoes, turnips, watercress.

(Do not use any fat or oil in the cooking of these vegetables.)

These are referred to as 'free' vegetables throughout this book and further ideas for making good use of them can be found in 'free' soups and 'free' salads in the Recipes section (pages 55-57).

Try to find a good herb and spice chart as herbs and spices transform humble salads and cooked vegetable dishes into something special.

## Optional Extras

Some recipes for cookies, tea breads and cakes (with their calorie values) can be found starting on page 94. These and bought 'treats' (see pages 107-108) can only be included in the plan if they are to be counted as part of the daily total. There is no room for such extras on the 1,000 calorie diet!

# Making The Plan Flexible

● Once your daily calorie intake is established you can then choose your meals, deciding when and how the calories are to be used up.

● Each day meals can be split and spread out to form smaller meals and snacks.

● Meals can be combined or doubled in quantity to increase your calorie total for the day.

● Once you have worked out the essentials for

your diet, you can include biscuits, cakes or snacks, whether home-made or bought, if they can be part of your total calorie intake for that day.

● You may find that some ideas for a certain meal are suitable for another time of the day. For example, a yogurt and fruit breakfast can be another dessert, extra to the basic plan.

● Where the recipe is for just one person, the quantity can easily be increased to cater for other members of the family.

● The recipes for one person indicate the ingredients that 'count' calorie-wise so that you can vary how you use them.

● Using the appendix at the back of the book which lists the calorie values of the different foods, you can include other ingredients in a meal provided that you allow for them in your total daily intake.

● Throughout this book the 'approximate' number of calories is always referred to. It is hoped that this approach, as well as allowing you to include freely many vegetables in the diet, will give you the confidence and freedom to work out your day plan without becoming pre-occupied with individual calories.

## Meal Options

### Daily Allowance

Make ONE selection from *each* of the milk/yogurt, fat and fruit allowances.

**Milk or Yogurt** (Provides 100 cals approximately)

Select *one* from the following:

> ½ pint (285ml) skimmed milk
> or ½ pint (285ml) unsweetened soy milk
> or 7 ozs (200g) natural yogurt (low fat)
> or 1 oz (30g) dried skimmed milk powder (made up with water in the normal way)

(Try to buy vitamin D fortified milk or yogurt)

**Fat** (Provides 100 cals approximately)

Select *one* from the following:

> 1 oz (30g) low fat spread
> or ½ oz (15g) vegetable margarine
> or 2 teaspoons (10ml) vegetable oil

(This is your total fat allowance so use non-stick frying pans and bakeware in your cooking and fry without using fat at all)

**Fruit** (Provides 50 cals approximately)

Select *one* portion of fruit from the following:

> 1 apple, small banana, large grapefruit, orange, peach or pear
> or 4 plums, apricots or figs
> or ½ medium mango
> or 3 oz (85g) grapes or pineapple
> or 5 oz (140g) blackberries, blackcurrants, damsons or strawberries
> or 8 oz (225g) melon with skin
> or 10 oz (285g) loganberries or gooseberries

(Where a 'portion of fruit' is referred to in the book, one selection can be made from any of the above fruits)

## BREAKFAST

Each day choose at least ONE breakfast from the options below.

The breakfast options given here are quick and easy, as first thing in the morning tends to be a hectic time for most people. There are three basic types of breakfast — bread/toast, cereals, eggs, yogurt and cheese — and a wide range within each one so that if you happen to, say, usually have toast, you can still vary your breakfast.

The calorific value can be increased by doubling the quantity given, or by combining two or more of the different kinds of breakfast.

*Note*: Only the ingredients that count in terms of calories are listed with each meal option so that you can invent your own variation if you like or follow the suggestions given in the method.

### Bread/Toast

Keep to wholemeal, granary, oatmeal or muesli bread. It can be lightly microwaved or toasted.

Wholemeal rolls, baps, muffins and pitta bread make a change from loaves.

Use low fat spread from allowance where required.

Yeast extract can be used freely and 1 oz (30g) whole fruit jam provides around 35 calories.

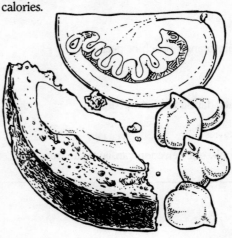

**150 cals approximately**

### 1. Toast with Yogurt Fruit Drink

*1 average slice bread*
*1 small carton natural yogurt*
*1 portion fruit from allowance*

Serve bread as toast with an accompanying drink of the yogurt and fruit liquidized together.

### 2. Toast with Chick-pea Spread

*1 average slice bread*
*3 oz (85g) cooked or tinned chick-peas*

Toast bread and spread with the chick-peas, mashed with a little soy sauce or yeast extract.

### 3. Toast with Fruity Cheese

*1 average slice bread*
*2 oz (55g) cottage cheese*
*2 or 3 dates, soaked in a little boiling water*

Toast bread and spread with cottage cheese, mashed with the dates.

Including 'free' vegetables, such as mushrooms or tomatoes, will make a larger, cooked breakfast and a salad will make it Middle Eastern!

Breakfast can be spread out to provide a midmorning snack.

Some breakfasts, e.g., yogurt and fruit, can provide another dessert during the day if your calorie allowance permits.

## 200 cals approximately

### 1. Toasted Cheese

*2 small slices bread*
*1 oz (30g) medium fat cheese*

Toast bread and top with grated cheese and chopped tomato. Grill.

### 2. Bread or Toast with Nut Butter

*2 small slices bread*
*½ oz (15g) nut butter or tahini*

Spread bread or toast with nut butter.

### 3. Muffin or Roll with Cottage Cheese and Jam

*1 muffin or roll*
*2 oz (55g) cottage cheese*
*½ oz (15g) whole fruit jam*

Toast muffin or roll halves and top with cottage cheese and jam mixture.

## 300 cals approximately

### 1. Toast with Spiced Beans

*2 average slices bread*
*4 oz (115g) baked beans*
*1 portion fruit*

Top toasted bread with baked beans, flavoured with a little curry powder.

### 2. Muffin or Roll with Nut Butter and Jam

*1 muffin or roll*
*½ oz (15g) nut butter or tahini*
*1 oz (30g) whole fruit jam*
*¼ pint (140ml) unsweetened fruit juice*

Toast roll or muffin and spread with nut butter or tahini paste and jam.

### 3. Toasted Pitta Bread with Cheese

*1 pitta bread*
*1 oz (30g) medium fat cheese*

Toast pitta bread and fill halves with grated cheese and chopped tomato or cooked mushrooms.

*(Breakfast Continued)*

## Cereals

Include only the wholemeal breakfast cereals in your diet — wheat, oat, barley, brown rice flakes, muesli base and muesli. Look for the manufactured brands with little or no added sugar.

Serve hot or cold and remember that the sweet spices add flavour and variety.

Soy milk, if used, should be unsweetened.

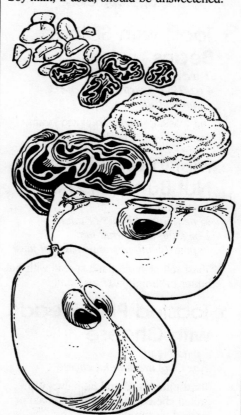

**150 cals approximately**

### 1. Fruit Porridge

*½ oz (15g) ground cereal*
*⅓ pint (200ml) skimmed or soy milk*
*½ oz (15g) dried fruit*

Simmer all the ingredients together with a little cinnamon until the cereal thickens. Serve hot or cold, adding milk from allowance if wanted.

### 2. Fruity Cottage Cheese with Crunchy Topping

*1 Weetabix*
*2 oz (55g) cottage cheese*
*3 fl oz (90ml) milk from allowance*
*1 oz (30g) dried apricots, soaked overnight*

Liquidize the cottage cheese and milk with the apricots and any soaking liquid. Pour into a dish and crumble Weetabix over the top.

### 3. Fruit and Shredded Wheat

*1 Shredded Wheat*
*4 fl oz (115ml) skimmed or soy milk*
*1 portion fruit*

Chop fruit, sprinkle on top of the Shredded Wheat and pour milk over. Add a few toasted seeds or some spice.

## 200 cals
### approximately

### 1. Nutty Cereal

*1 oz (30g) cereal*
*4 fl oz (115ml) skimmed or soy milk*
*½ oz (15g) toasted hazelnuts, chopped*
*   or ground*

Mix all the ingredients together.

### 2. Shredded Wheat and Yogurt

*1 Shredded Wheat*
*4 fl oz (115ml) fruit juice*
*1 carton natural yogurt*

Heat fruit juice and add a little ground ginger. Pour over the Shredded Wheat and top with yogurt.

### 3. Fruit Muesli with Yogurt

*1 oz (30g) muesli*
*1 carton natural yogurt*
*½ oz (15g) dried prunes, soaked*

Mix all ingredients together, along with a little toasted coconut.

## 300 cals
### approximately

### 1. Fruity Cereal

*2 oz (55g) cereal*
*⅓ pint (200ml) skimmed or soy milk*
*1 portion fruit, chopped*

Mix all ingredients together.

### 2. Weetabix with Fruit

*2 Weetabix*
*⅓ pint (200ml) skimmed or soy milk*
*½ oz (15g) dried fruit*
*¼ pint (140ml) unsweetened fruit juice*

Sprinkle fruit over the Weetabix, add milk and serve with fruit juice.

### 3. Fruit and Nut Granola with Yogurt

*1 oz (30g) granola-type cereal*
*1 portion fruit, chopped or grated as*
*   necessary*
*½ oz (15g) toasted nuts, chopped*
*1 carton natural yogurt*

Either mix all the ingredients together or top the fruit and yogurt with the granola and nuts.

## Eggs, Yogurt and Cheese

Eggs can be boiled, poached, fried in a non-stick pan, scrambled or made into an omelette using milk or yogurt from allowance if required.

Buy natural yogurt or make your own. Use it as a base to which fruit, nuts and cereal can be added, or as a topping. Use herbs and spices to add variety.

**150 cals
approximately**

### 1. Soufflé Omelette

*1 egg*
*1 average slice wholemeal bread*

Make a soufflé omelette by separating the egg and yolk, adding any left-over cooked 'free' vegetables to the beaten yolk and folding in the firm beaten egg whites. Fry in a pan, finishing off under the grill.

### 2. Yogurt and Cottage Cheese with Fruit

*1 carton natural yogurt*
*1 oz (30g) cottage cheese*
*1 portion fruit*

Liquidize yogurt and cottage cheese and mix with chopped or grated fruit and some spices.

### 3. Bean Fritters

*1 egg*
*3 oz (85g) tinned baked or barbeque or chilli beans*

Make bean fritters by mashing beans, mixing with beaten egg and dropping spoonfuls in to a frying pan. Cook on both sides and serve with grilled tomatoes or mushrooms.

<table>
<tr><td>200 cals<br>approximately</td><td>300 cals<br>approximately</td></tr>
</table>

## 1. Poached Egg with Savoury Yogurt

*1 egg*
*1 carton natural yogurt*
*1 portion fruit*

Poach egg, place in yogurt, flavoured with a little crushed garlic and seasoning. Sprinkle with a little paprika.

## 2. Curried Potato Cakes

*1 egg*
*5 oz (140g) cooked potato, mashed*

Make some curried potato cakes by mixing the mashed potato with finely chopped onion and/or tomato, curry powder and the beaten egg, adding seasoning to taste. Drop spoonfuls into the pan and fry both sides. Serve with grilled mushrooms.

## 3. Watercress Quark with a Roll

*¼ pint (140ml) skimmed milk*
*2 oz (55g) quark*
*1 small wholemeal roll*

Liquidize the milk and quark with ½ bunch watercress (save a sprig or two to garnish) and add lemon juice and seasoning to taste. Garnish with some chopped watercress and serve with the roll.

## 1. Egg and Bread Fritters

*1 egg*
*2 average slices wholemeal bread*
*¼ pint (140ml) unsweetened fruit juice*

Make egg and bread fritters by soaking triangles of the bread in the seasoned beaten egg. Fry both sides and top with tomato slices and a sprinkle of chopped parsley to serve.

## 2. Fruit and Nuts with Yogurt

*1 carton natural yogurt*
*1 oz (30g) dried apricots* } *soaked*
*½ oz (15g) dried fruit* } *overnight*
*1 oz (30g) nuts, chopped*

Pile the mixture of fruit and nuts on to the yogurt.

## 3. Cheese Whirls with Tomato and Roll

*1 egg*
*1½ oz (45g) medium fat cheese*
*1 small wholemeal roll*

Make a cheese omelette, sprinkle with a few toasted sesame seeds while cooking and roll up. Slice to form whirls and pile on to lightly grilled tomato slices. Serve with the roll.

## LIGHT/EASY MEALS

Each day, either choose ONE meal from any of the options below or TWO meals if you are shor of time and energy instead of including a More Effort/Family Meal in your plan.

Whenever possible, try to accompany this meal with 'free' vegetables — preferably as a salad o just lightly cooked.

Double the quantity or combine different meals to increase the calorific value.

*Note*: Only the ingredients that have a calorific value are listed with each option so that you ca either invent your own variation or follow the suggestions given in the method.

### Sandwiches and Rolls

Bread can be wholemeal, oatmeal, muesli or granary and in the form of a loaf, roll, bap or pitta bread. The sandwich or roll can be fresh or toasted and as a round or open with a topping.

'Free' vegetables can make a side salad or be included in the sandwich, chopped or grated as necessary (see page 11 for suggestions).

Use low fat spread from allowance where required.

A sprinking of herbs or spices or spreading a little yeast extract, tomato purée, mustard or horseradish sauce will add extra flavour.

Left-over cooked vegetables, such as cauliflower, broccoli, carrot and parsnip, can be mashed and mixed in with the other ingredients to make a more interesting spread.

**250 cals
approximately**

### 1. Butter Bean and Olive Sandwich

*2 average slices bread or 1 bap or roll
3 oz (85g) tinned or cooked butter beans
3 black olives, stoned*

Mash beans with the olives and a little lemon juice and seasoning to use as a spread.

### 2. Nutmeat Toasted Sandwich

*2 average slices bread
2 oz (55g) tinned nutmeat*

Lightly spread bread with yeast extract, and make a sandwich with slices of nutmeat and chopped tomato, then toast.

Soups made with 'free' vegetables can be found on pages 55-56. These do not have to be counted and can add another course to your meal.

Some breakfasts (pages 14-19) may be combined with some of these meals to increase calorific value, e.g., yogurt or bread additions, especially if the day's dessert allowance is being saved for the evening or other meal or a snack.

| 300 cals approximately | 400 cals approximately |
|---|---|

**300 cals approximately**

## 1. Chick-pea-and-Mushroom-filled Pitta Bread

*1 pitta bread*
*3 oz (85g) tinned or cooked chick-peas*

Cook some sliced button mushrooms, chopped onions and parsley in a little soy sauce. Add chick-peas to heat through, mash and fill toasted pitta bread halves.

## 2. Toasted Cheese, Date and Celery Sandwich

*2 average slices bread*
*3 oz (85g) curd cheese*
*½ oz (15g) chopped dates*

Mix together cheese, dates, celery and seasoning, fill sandwich and toast.

**400 cals approximately**

## 1. Nut Butter and Banana Sandwich

*4 average slices bread*
*1 small banana*
*½ oz (15g) nut butter or tahini*

Mash banana with the nut butter to use as a spread. Add bean shoots to the filling.

## 2. Fried-bean-filled Pitta Bread

*1 pitta bread*
*3 oz (85g) tinned chilli beans*
*1 oz (30g) medium fat cheese, grated*

Mash beans and mix with grated cheese and chopped parsley. Fry until the mixture is hot and the cheese has melted. Fill toasted pitta bread pockets with the mixture, adding chopped 'free' salad vegetables.

*(Light/Easy Meals Continued)*

**250 cals**
**approximately**

### 3. Mini Pizzas

*1 roll or bap*
*1½ oz (45g) medium fat cheese*

Toast roll halves, top with a mixture of
the grated cheese, chopped tomato,
spring onion, dried oregano and
seasoning. Grill topping.

**300 cals**
**approximately**

### 3. Creamy Egg Sandwich

*3 average slices bread*
*1 hard-boiled egg*
*1 tablespoon natural yogurt*

Mash egg with yogurt, add chopped
spring onion and a little mustard. Use
as a filling for one layer of a three-
tiered sandwich, and 'free' salad
ingredients for the other.

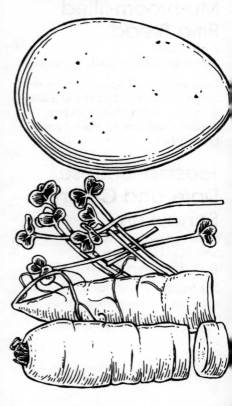

**400 cals**
**approximately**

3. # Avocado and Cottage Cheese Sandwich

*3 average slices bread*
*2 oz (55g) avocado, mashed*
*2 oz (55g) cottage cheese*

Make a three-tiered sandwich by spreading mashed avocado with a little lemon juice and chopped tomato for one layer, and cottage cheese, watercress and a few toasted sesame seeds for the other.

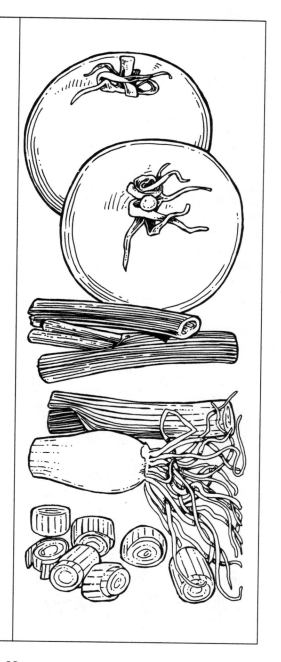

*(Light/Easy Meals Continued)*

## Salads

In this section, the ingredients that have a significant calorific value are given and you can choose any 'free' vegetables to complete the salad, although suggestions are given in the method. Some salad suggestions can be found, starting on page 57, and the meal option you have chosen from the table can be used as a topping, served with the side salad or you can mix everything up together.

Use mustard and cress, chopped parsley, chives, red, green or yellow peppers and toasted seeds as a garnish.

Many of the meal options have no herbs or spices included. This is so you can select your own and experiment.

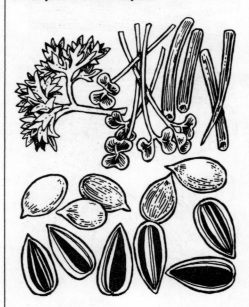

**250 cals approximately**

### 1. Fruit and Cottage Cheese

*1 peach, pear or apple*
*4 oz (115g) cottage cheese*
*½ oz (15g) chopped nuts*
*½ oz (15g) dried fruit*

Cut fruit in half, stone or core and arrange on a green salad. Mix the cottage cheese with the dried fruit and nuts and pile it on top.

### 2. Egg, Broad Beans and Yogurt

*1 hard-boiled egg*
*4 oz (115g) cooked or tinned broad beans*
*1 carton natural yogurt*
*1 portion fruit*

Chop egg, mix with the beans, natural yogurt, spring onion and mint. Serve with a crunchy 'free' side salad which can include the fruit portion.

### 3. Banana and Tofu

*4 oz (115g) silken tofu*
*1 banana*
*½ oz (15g) chopped walnuts*
*1 oz (30g) sweet corn*

Blend or mash the tofu and banana with a little lemon juice. Mix with the nuts, sweet corn and other 'free' salad vegetables, such as bean shoots, peppers and radishes.

## 300 cals approximately

# Cheese and Cracked Wheat

*1 oz (30g) cracked wheat, soaked and lightly cooked*
*2 oz (55g) medium fat cheese, cubed*
*1 portion fruit*

Mix the wheat with some chopped tomatoes, parsley, fresh mint, a squeeze of lemon juice, seasoning and the cubes of cheese. Serve with a crunchy 'free' salad, which can include the portion of fruit.

# Chick-peas with Tahini Dressing

*5 oz (140g) cooked or tinned chick-peas*
*½ oz (15g) tahini*
*½ carton natural yogurt*
*1 portion fruit*

Mix chick-peas, with some 'free' salad ingredients, such as chopped peppers, grated courgettes, chopped spring onion and fresh coriander. Pile on to a bed of lettuce or watercress and pour over this a dressing of the yogurt blended with tahini, a little lemon juice and seasoning.

# Stuffed Pepper or Tomatoes

*4 oz (115g) curd cheese*
*1 oz (30g) chopped dates*
*½ oz (15g) roasted almonds, chopped*

Mix the cheese, dates and nuts together with some chopped celery, spring onion or chives. Fill a deseeded red pepper or tomatoes with the cheese, nut and celery mixture and serve on a bed of green salad made from 'free' vegetables.

## 400 cals approximately

# 1. Lentils and Rice

*6 oz (170g) tinned or cooked continental lentils*
*5 oz (140g) cooked brown rice*
*1 oz (30g) dried apricots, chopped*

Mix together the lentils, rice and chopped apricots with some onion, tomatoes, green pepper, a little dessicated coconut, a squeeze of lemon juice and seasoning. Serve with a leafy green 'free' salad.

# 2. Beetroot, Apple and Yogurt

*1 carton natural yogurt*
*2 oz (55g) raw beetroot, grated*
*1 apple, grated*
*1 oz (30g) roasted hazelnuts, chopped*
*1 wholemeal roll*

Mix the first five ingredients together adding a little chopped onion, a squeeze of lemon juice and seasoning. Serve with the roll and a mixed salad of 'free' vegetables.

# 3. Nut Balls

*2 oz (55g) nuts, ground*
*1½ oz (45g) fresh wholemeal breadcrumbs*

Mix the nuts, breadcrumbs and some chopped chives together. Dissolve a little yeast extract in 2 tablespoons of hot water and add to the nut and breadcrumb mixture, along with seasoning. Make small, firm balls with the mixture and coat them with toasted sesame seeds or wheatgerm and pile on to a mixed salad of 'free' vegetables.

## Jacket Potatoes

A 6 oz (170g) potato will need about 1 hour at Gas Mark 6, 200°C or 400°F (a shorter time if skewered). Microwaved it will need about 4-5 minutes on high power.

It can be served on its own with low fat spread from the daily allowance, with the meal option chosen, forming part of a salad; or it can be topped or the potato scooped out and mixed with the ingredients to be piled back in, as suggested in the table.

Use 'free' vegetables, cooked, chopped or grated to extend the topping or filling.

Of course, the potato can be served in a different way to accompany the other ingredients in the meal option.

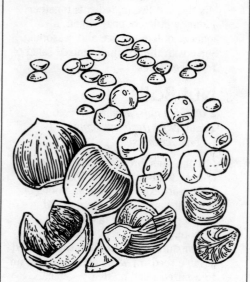

**250 cals approximately**

### 1. Egg and Sweet Corn Topping

*6 oz (170g) jacket potato*
*1 egg*
*1 oz (30g) cooked or tinned sweet corn*

Beat the egg, add the sweet corn, some chopped onion, peppers or tomatoes, some herbs and seasoning. Scramble and top the potato.

### 2. Creamy Hazelnut Topping

*6 oz (170g) jacket potato*
*2 oz (55g) silken tofu*
*½ oz (15g) hazelnuts, ground*

Blend tofu and hazelnuts, add a little chopped spring onion, a dash of soy sauce and a little thyme and seasoning. Top the potato with the mixture and garnish with chopped fresh parsley.

### 3. Cottage Cheese and Fruit Topping

*6 oz (170g) jacket potato*
*4 oz (115g) cottage cheese with pineapple*

Mix the cottage cheese with some chopped chives or spring onion and a few toasted sesame seeds. Top the potato.

| 300 cals approximately | 400 cals approximately |
|---|---|

## 1. Tahini Topping

*6 oz (170g) jacket potato*
*3 oz (85g) cottage cheese*
*½ oz (15g) tahini*

Blend the cottage cheese and tahini, adding some chopped celery and herbs. Pile on to the potato and grill.

## 2. Lentil and Cheese Topping

*6 oz (170g) jacket potato*
*3 oz (85g) cooked lentils*
*1 oz (30g) medium fat cheese*

Mash the lentils, mix with the cheese, a little yeast extract, some chopped tomato and seasoning. Heat through and pile on to the potato. Garnish with some cress or chopped chives. Alternatively, scoop out the potato, mix with the lentils and cheese and pile back into the potato shell.

## 3. Bean and Vegetable Topping

*8 oz (225g) jacket potato*
*4 oz (115g) tinned barbeque or chilli beans*

Mix the beans with any left-over 'free' vegetables. Heat through and pile on to the potato. Sprinkle some toasted seeds over the top.

## 1. Hummus Topping

*6 oz (170g) jacket potato*
*4 oz (115g) cooked or tinned chick-peas*
*½ oz (15g) tahini*
*1 portion fruit*

Blend the chick-peas with the tahini, a squeeze of lemon juice and a little crushed garlic, cumin and chilli powder. Top the potato and garnish with chopped fresh parsley.

## 2. Grilled Cheese and Apple Topping

*8 oz (225g) jacket potato*
*2 oz (55g) medium fat cheese*
*1 apple*

Grate both the cheese and apple, add some seasoning and pile on to the potato. Grill until the cheese is bubbling.

## 3. Nutty Coleslaw Topping

*8 oz (225g) jacket potato*
*2 oz (55g) curd cheese*
*1 oz (30g) roasted hazelnuts, chopped*

Blend the curd cheese with a squeeze of lemon juice and seasoning. Make a coleslaw using cabbage, carrot, onion and chopped fresh mint and mix with nuts and curd cheese dressing. Top the potato.

*(Light/Easy Meals Continued)*

## Simple Savouries

All of these meals are easy and quick to prepare — in fact they can be ready to eat in less than half an hour.

When cooked vegetables are included they can either be freshly cooked or leftovers (which may need to be heated through first).

As these meals are all lightly cooked, make use of fresh herbs (lovage, parsley, coriander, sage, thyme, rosemary, basil, etc.) to give a variety of flavours to any one dish.

A fruit portion can be part of an accompanying side salad, the dessert, or can be liquidized with milk or yogurt from the daily allowance to make a drink.

**250 cals approximately**

### 1. Broccoli with Cottage Cheese

*8 oz (225g) broccoli or cauliflower*
*4 oz (115g) cottage cheese*
*1 small wholemeal roll*
*1 portion fruit*

Chop the broccoli or cauliflower and pile into a pan along with the cottage cheese, chopped onion, a little nutmeg and seasoning. Cook gently until the vegetables are tender and the liquid has been absorbed. Garnish with a little chopped red pepper or tomato and serve with the wholemeal roll.

### 2. Pulse Patties

*6 oz (170g) cooked or tinned beans or lentils*
*1 oz (30g) fresh wholemeal breadcrumbs*

Mash the beans or lentils with the breadcrumbs and mix with chopped celery, peppers, mushrooms, spring onion, parsley or coriander, lemon juice, cumin powder and seasoning. Form the mixture into two patties, coat with wheatgerm, bran or sesame seeds and fry on both sides.

## 300 cals
### approximately

### 1. Nut Burgers

*1½ oz (45g) nuts, ground*
*1 oz (30g) fresh wholemeal*
  *breadcrumbs*

Mix nuts, breadcrumbs, grated or chopped 'free' vegetables, chopped spring onion, herbs and seasoning with 1-2 fl oz (30-60ml) hot water with a little yeast extract dissolved in it. Form into two burgers, coat with wheatgerm, bran or sesame seeds and fry on both sides.

### 2. Spiced Beans and Pasta

*1 oz (30g) wholewheat pasta*
*6 oz (170g) cooked or tinned beans*

Empty a small tin of tomatoes into a pan along with the pasta, beans, a chopped onion (plus carrot and celery if liked), ½ teaspoon cinnamon or allspice and seasoning. Simmer until the pasta is cooked and the sauce has thickened. Garnish with the chopped parsley.

## 400 cals
### approximately

### 1. Sweet-and-sour Vegetables with Tofu

*2 oz (55g) cooked or tinned sweet corn*
*2 oz (55g) frozen peas*
*1 oz (30g) toasted almonds*
*3 oz (85g) pineapple, drained from*
  *natural juice*
*4 oz (115g) plain firm tofu*

Stir-fry some finely chopped 'free' vegetables, the sweet corn, peas and almonds in some soy sauce and a little water or stock until the vegetables are just tender. Add the pineapple to heat through and serve topped with chunks of fried tofu.

### 2. Pease Pudding and Hazelnut Cheese Grill

*5 oz (140g) cooked split peas or tinned*
  *pease pudding*
*1 oz (30g) toasted hazelnuts, chopped*
*2 oz (55g) medium fat cheese, grated*

Mash the peas with half of the hazelnuts, chopped spring onion or chives, fresh herbs, a little soy sauce and pepper. Place half the mixture in a shallow dish, cover with thin slices of tomato then the rest of the peas. Top with the grated cheese mixed with rest of the hazelnuts and grill to heat through and crisp the topping.

# Simply Slim

| 250 cals approximately | 300 cals approximately |
|---|---|

## 3. Creamy Egg and Nut Curry

*1 carton natural yogurt*
*½ oz (15g) roasted peanuts*
*1 egg, hard-boiled*

Stir some cooked 'free' vegetables in a pan with some curry powder and a little stock, to heat through, and to coat the vegetables with the spice. Add yogurt and peanuts, mix well and gently warm. Serve, topped with egg wedges and a sprinkle of chopped parsley.

## 3. Crispy Cheese-topped Vegetables

*2½ oz (70g) medium fat cheese, grated*
*2 wholemeal crispbreads*
*1 portion fruit*

Place some hot, cooked 'free' vegetables, which have been mixed with chopped fresh herbs, into a shallow dish. Sprinkle with soy sauce and top with a mixture of the grated cheese and crumbled crispbread. Grill to brown the topping.

**400 cals
approximately**

## 3. Fruit and Spice Millet

*2 oz (55g) millet
1 oz (30g) raisins, sultanas or currants
½ oz (15g) prunes, chopped
4 oz (115g) cottage cheese*

Place millet in four times its volume of water, along with the raisins, chopped prunes, a little cinnamon and a clove. Cook until 'fluffy', fork and serve with the cottage cheese.

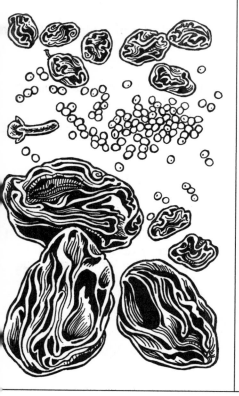

## MORE EFFORT/FAMILY MEALS

Each day choose either ONE meal from any of the options below or TWO meals if you have mo⟨
time, energy and enthusiasm instead of including a Light/Easy Meal in your day plan.

In the following tables are the names of the dishes which will serve four people (unless otherwi⟨
stated), giving the particular calorie total per portion that you can see heading each colum⟨

Certain meals contain two dishes, which need to be served together to ensure the right numb⟨
of calories (and, in some cases, the right amount of protein per serving). The page number ⟨
the recipe(s) is also given.

| 250 cals approximately per portion | 300 cals approximately per portion |
|---|---|
| **Burgers, Rissoles and Fritters** | |
| 1. Tofu and Vegetable Slices (page 60) | 1. Soya Bean and Hazelnut Fritters (page 68) |
| 2. Spinach and Cheese Fritters (page 61) | 2. Cauliflower and Almond Burge⟨ with Corn and Peas (page 68) |
| 3. Potato and Mushroom Cutlets (page 61) | 3. Watercress and Potato Burgers (page 69) |
| **Stuffed Vegetables** | |
| 1. Cheese-stuffed Courgettes (page 61) | 1. Nutty Stuffed Tomatoes with Pepper Sauce and Bean Salad (page 69) |
| 2. Potato-stuffed Mushrooms with Spiced Vegetables and Beans (page 62) | 2. Cheese-and-apple-stuffed Peppers with Tomato and Egg Scramble (page 70) |
| 3. Mushroom-stuffed Aubergines with Cottage Cheese Salad (page 62) | 3. Cheese-and-nut-stuffed Onions with Minted Bean Ratatouille (page 70) |

ny of the meals can be served with a bowl of vegetables from the 'free' list, either as a salad, casserole, stew, stir-fried or cooked very simply. Occasionally, particularly suitable vegetables ay be suggested.

ouble the quantity or combine different meals to increase the total calorific value or include dessert.

| 400 cals approximately per portion | 500 cals approximately per portion |
|---|---|
| Lentil and Millet Squares with Tomato Sauce (page 76) | 1. Peanut, Sesame and Apple Burgers with Curried Salad (page 85) |
| Curried Cereal and Cheese Balls with Stir-fried Vegetabes (page 76) | 2. Coconut and Rice Squares with Mixed Bean Salad (page 85) |
| Spiced Rice and Pea Burgers (page 77) | 3. Dolly's Burgers with Tomato and Potatoes in Cheese Sauce (page 86) |
| Aubergine-stuffed Tomatoes with Lentils and Spinach (page 77) | 1. Rice-stuffed Cabbage Leaves Baked in Coconut Sauce with Fried Tofu (page 86) |
| Bean-and-rice-stuffed Marrow with Sesame Parsnips (page 78) | 2. Cracked-wheat-stuffed Peppers with Mixed Vegetable Salad and Peanut Sauce (page 87) |
| Spiced Potato-stuffed Marrow with Cheese-topped Cabbage Masala (page 78) | 3. Chick-pea-stuffed Aubergines with Cauliflower in Tahini Sauce (page 88) |

# Simply Slim

| 250 cals approximately per portion | 300 cals approximately per portion |
|---|---|
| **Bakes, Savouries and Roasts** | |
| 1. Broccoli Bake with Orange and Nut Celery (page 63) | 1. Red Kidney Bean and Walnut Roast (page 71) |
| 2. Savoury Egg and Rice Loaf with Braised Cabbage (page 63) | 2. Gingered Lentil and Pineapple Loaf with Tofu-dressed Mixed Salad (page 71) |
| 3. Carrot and Watercress Loaf with Creamy Mushrooms (page 64) | 3. Vegetable and Oat Pie (page 72) |
| **Pastries, Pies and Pizzas** | |
| 1. Celeriac-filled Buckwheat Pancakes (page 64) | 1. Spiced Lentil Flan Serves 6 (page 72) |
| 2. Cauliflower-filled Yogurt Pancakes with Cumin Courgettes (page 65) | 2. Chick-pea Pancakes with Smoked Aubergine (page 73) |
| 3. Vegetable-filled Pancakes with Rosemary Tomatoes (page 66) | 3. Quick Pan Pizza Serves 2 (page 73) |
| **Casseroles, Stews and Vegetable Dishes** | |
| 1. Spinach Roulade with Creamed Carrot and Swede (page 66) | 1. Spiced Lentils and Rice (page 74) |
| 2. Curried Vegetables and Lentils (page 67) | 2. Butter Bean and Potato Goulash (page 74) |
| 3. Chick-pea Casserole (page 67) | 3. Vegetable Moussaka with Citrus Parsnips (page 75) |

| 400 cals approximately per portion | 500 cals approximately per portion |
|---|---|
| Cheese and Courgette Charlotte with Orange, Raisin and Watercress Salad (page 79) | 1. Courgette, Tofu and Nut Bake with Creamy Brussels Sprouts (page 88) |
| Sunflower and Sesame Loaf with New Potatoes in Spinach Sauce (page 80) | 2. Mary's Chick-pea Savoury with Mushroom Sauce (page 89) |
| Corn and Tomato Bake with Spicy Peas (page 80) | 3. Curried Mushroom Ring with Potato and Cheese Layer (page 90) |
| Nut Pastry Mushroom Flan (page 81) | 1. Pasties with Cauliflower and Peanut Salad (page 90) |
| Spinach and Cheese Pie (page 81) | 2. Sweet Corn Pizza with Minted Courgette and Yogurt Salad (page 91) |
| Yogurt Scone Ratatouille Pizza with Bean and Nut Salad (page 82) | 3. Mexican-bean-topped Corn Pizza (page 92) |
| Macaroni Cheese and Vegetable Casserole with Ginger and Garlic Carrots Serves 6 (page 82) | 1. Mushroom and Cashew Nut Rice (page 92) |
| Vegetable and Millet Pie with Cucumber and Herbs (page 83) | 2. Fruity Bean Stew with Wholemeal Rolls (page 93) |
| Cauliflower, Leek and Hazelnut Casserole with Red Kidney Bean and Courgette Salad (page 84) | 3. Aubergine and Red Kidney Bean Casserole with Spinach Rice (page 93) |

## DESSERTS

Each day choose ONE of the dessert options below. Only the ingredients with significant calorie are listed with each option so that you can easily vary the recipe if you want to (ingredients with negligible calorific values appear in the method).

They are all fruit-based, providing fibre and sweetness without added sugar. Dried fruit is frequently soaked as this increases the quantity without adding very many calories.

### 100 cals approximately

### 1. Mango and Cardamom Cream

*½ medium mango, peeled*
*½ small carton natural yogurt*

Liquidize the mango, yogurt and the seeds of 2 cardamom pods in a blender. Serve chilled.

### 2. Pear in Red Wine

*1 pear, cored and sliced*
*2½ fl oz (75ml) red wine*

Simmer the pear slices with a pinch each of ginger, cinnamon and cloves, in the wine until just tender. Serve hot or cold.

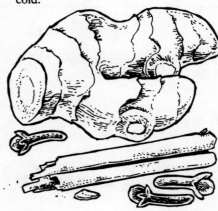

### 150 cals approximately

### 1. Rum and Raisin Cream

*½ oz (15g) raisins*
*2 teaspoons rum*
*1 small carton natural yogurt*
*1 oz (30g) quark or cottage cheese*

Soak the raisins in the rum and a little water overnight. Liquidize all the ingredients together and serve.

### 2. Baked Apples or Pears with Fruit Filling

*1 8 oz (225g) cooking apple or pear*
*½ oz (15g) dates, chopped*
*½ oz (15g) raisins, sultanas or currants*

Soak the dried fruit in a little water overnight together with a pinch each cinnamon, nutmeg and allspice. Pack into the cored apple or pear. Wrap in foil and bake at Gas Mark 4, 180°C or 350°F for 30-40 minutes or until tender.

ᵐe breakfast options on page 16 are suitable as alternative desserts. Garnish them with ground, ᵢked or chopped nuts or toasted coconut or sesame seeds.

ᵗe quantities given for the desserts below are for a single portion but the amounts can easily ᵗ increased if you are catering for others as well. On such occasions you may want to choose ᵗecipe from the Treats section on pages 94-99, as a dessert, but you need to make sure that you ᵢn include the calories of your portion in your daily total.

### 200 cals
### approximately

## Prunes with Coconut Sauce

*2 oz (55g) prunes, stoned*
*¾ oz (20g) creamed coconut*

Soak prunes overnight in sufficient cold tea to cover. Simmer until soft, drain off the liquid and beat it into the coconut cream to make a sauce. Serve the prunes hot or cold with the sauce.

## Fruit and Nut Cream

*1 portion fresh fruit*
*1 oz (30g) almonds, ground*

Chop fruit and stew in a little water and lemon juice until soft. Liquidize with the nuts and a little sweet spice to make a cream.

### 250 cals
### approximately

## 1. Almond-stuffed Peach

*1 large fresh peach*
*1 oz (30g) almonds, ground*
*1 teaspoon honey*

Cut the peach in half and stone. Beat the honey into the almonds to make a stiff paste and form two balls with the mixture. Press a ball into each peach half and bake at Gas Mark 4, 180°C or 350°F for about 20 minutes or until the peach is just tender.

## 2. Tutti-frutti

*4 oz (115g) quark or tofu*
*4 glacé cherries, chopped*
*1 oz (30g) mixed fruit*
*1 oz (30g) whole fruit marmalade*

Mix all the ingredients together and chill.

## 100 cals approximately

### 3. Apricot or Prune Fool

*1 oz (30g) dried apricots or prunes*
*2 oz (55g) quark or tofu*

Soak the apricots or prunes overnight and blend with the quark or tofu (remove prune stones first).

### 4. Fruit Mousse

*4 oz (115g) soft, sweet fruit*
*1 peach, pear or small banana*
*1 egg white*

Stew the fruit together, purée, cool and stir in the stiffly beaten egg white.

## 150 cals approximately

### 3. Carrot, Fruit and Nut Dessert

*4 oz (115g) carrots, finely grated*
*5 fl oz (140ml) skimmed milk*
*½ oz (15g) raisins*
*¼ oz (7g) almonds, ground*

Simmer all the ingredients together with the crushed seeds of 2 cardamom pods and ¼ teaspoon cinnamon. Serve hot when the mixture has thickened and reduced or leave to cool.

### 4. Apricot and Pineapple Crumble

*1 oz (30g) dried apricots, soaked*
*4 oz (115g) fresh pineapple or tinned,*
    *drained from natural juice*
*1 wholemeal biscuit, crumbled*

Chop the apricots and simmer with the pineapple in any soaking liquid or a little water. When the apricots are soft, spoon the mixture into a dish and top with the biscuit crumbs.

|  |  |
|---|---|
| **200 cals**<br>**approximately** | **250 cals**<br>**approximately** |

## 3. Apricot and Oatmeal Layer

*1 oz (30g) dried apricots*
*¼ oz (7g) hazelnuts, finely chopped*
*½ oz (15g) coarse, pinhead oatmeal*
*⅓ pint (200ml) skimmed milk*

Soak the apricots overnight. Soak separately the nuts, oatmeal and the crushed seeds of 2 cardamom pods in the milk overnight. Simmer the oatmeal mixture gently to thicken, then cool. Mash the apricots and layer with the oatmeal in an individual dish, finishing with the oatmeal. Sprinkle some cinnamon over the top.

## 4. Mini Fruit Cheesecake

*3 oz (85g) low fat cheese or quark*
*1 oz (30g) prunes, soaked, stoned and*
*    chopped*
*½ oz (15g) raisins, soaked*
*1 small wholemeal biscuit, crumbled*

Beat a little lemon juice into the cheese, followed by the chopped fruit, raisins and ¼ teaspoon mixed spice. Press into a shallow dish, with the biscuit crumbs firmly pushed down on the top. Leave overnight in the fridge and turn out.

## 3. Banana and Date Sandwich

*2 oz (55g) dates*
*1 small banana, cut lengthways*
*1 small carton natural or soy yogurt*

Heat the dates with a little water until boiling, leave to cool and mash. Use half of the date mixture to sandwich together the two halves of the banana, the rest to mix in with the yogurt to pour over the top of the banana.

## 4. Fruit and Nut Semolina

*¼ pint (140ml) skimmed milk*
*½ oz (15g) wholewheat semolina*
*1 oz (30g) raisins*
*3 glacé cherries, chopped*
*¼ oz (7g) flaked almonds, toasted*

Heat the milk to boiling point and then sprinkle in the semolina, stirring continuously. Add the raisins, cherries and ¼ teaspoon cinnamon and simmer gently, stirring all the time until the semolina is quite cooked (about 10 minutes). Either serve hot, topped with the almonds, or pour quickly into a cold, wetted dish, and leave to cool, chill and then empty the nuts over the turned out mould.

### 100 cals approximately

## 5. Spiced Fruit

*1 apple or pear, grated*
*½ oz (15g) raisins or sultanas*
*½ oz dried apricots, chopped*

Mix fruit with a squeeze of lemon juice, ¼ teaspoon sweet spice and leave to soak overnight. Sprinkle some dessicated coconut over the top to serve.

## 6. Orange in Orange Flower Water

*1 orange*
*½ oz (15g) raisins*
*2 fl oz (60ml) unsweetened orange juice*

Peel the orange, chop the segments and place in a bowl with the raisins and orange juice, mixed with a few drops of orange flower water. Leave in the fridge for a few hours, if possible, and serve sprinkled with cinnamon.

### 150 cals approximately

## 5. Apple and Fig Cream with Ginger

*1 apple*
*2 small dried figs, soaked and chopped*
*½ small carton natural yogurt*

Halve and core the apple. Liquidize one half with the figs, yogurt, a little lemon juice and ¼ teaspoon ground ginger. Mix with the remaining half of the apple, grated.

## 6. Hazelnut and Fruit Dessert

*1 oz (30g) hazelnuts, ground*
*1 portion sweet, fresh fruit*

Liquidize nuts, fruit, ¼ teaspoon sweet spice and a little lemon juice. If liked, add some water to achieve the desired consistency.

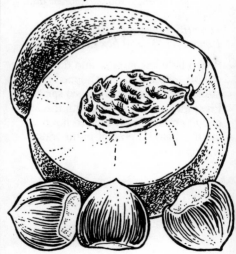

| 200 cals approximately | 250 cals approximately |
|---|---|

## 5. Crispy-topped Fruit

*1 portion sweet fresh or frozen fruit,*
  *chopped*
*½ oz (15g) wholewheat flakes*
*½ oz (15g) hazelnuts, chopped*
*1 teaspoon vegetable oil*

Stew the chopped fruit in a little water until just tender. Mix the flakes, nuts and vegetable oil together and top the hot fruit. Grill to crisp the top.

## 6. Marzipan-filled Fruit

*3 dried apricots or 2 dates or 2 large*
  *prunes*
*1 oz (30g) almonds, ground*
*1 teaspoon clear honey*

Prepare fruit by halving and removing stones, where necessary. Make the marzipan by beating the honey and a drop of almond essence into the almonds. Make 2 or 3 balls and press a ball into one half of the fruit, pressing the other half on top, repeating for the rest of the fruit.

## 5. Apricot and Cashew Dessert

*2 oz (55g) dried apricots, soaked*
*1 oz (30g) cashew nuts, ground*
*1 fl oz (30ml) unsweetened fruit juice*

Simmer the apricots in their soaking liquid until soft and then mash them. Mix the nuts with the fruit juice. Spoon the apricots and nut cream into a glass to form layers.

## 6. Fruit Salad with Granola

*5 oz (140g) fruit salad, tinned in*
  *natural juice*
*½ small carton natural yogurt*
*1 oz (30g) granola cereal*
*¼ oz (7g) dessicated coconut*

Top the fruit salad with the yogurt, followed by the granola and finally the coconut.

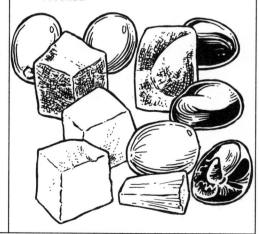

| 100 cals approximately | 150 cals approximately |
|---|---|

### 7. Berry and Orange Crush

*4 oz (115g) strawberries or raspberries*
*¼ pint (140ml) unsweetened orange juice*

Put fruit and juice in a blender with 1 or 2 ice cubes. Serve immediately.

### 8. Banana with Blackcurrant

*5 oz (140g) blackcurrants*
*1 small banana cut in 3 lengthways*

Stew the blackcurrants with one third of the banana, chopped, and a little water. Purée, and cool. Meanwhile, sprinkle lemon juice over the remaining pieces of banana. Serve with the blackcurrant purée poured over the banana slices.

### 7. Banana Rice Pudding

*1 small banana, sliced*
*½ oz (15g) brown rice flakes*
*¼ pint (140ml) skimmed milk*

Simmer all ingredients together until the mixture thickens. Sprinkle with nutmeg to serve.

### 8. Fruit Salad

*2 oz (55g) red grapes, deseeded*
*1 orange, peeled and chopped*
*1 small pear, cored and chopped*
*1 green apple, cored and chopped*

Mix fruit together and add a few drops of dry sherry.

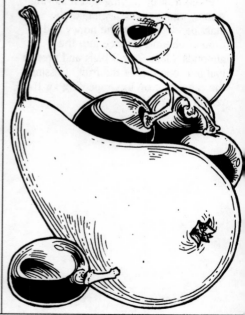

**200 cals**
**approximately**

## 7. Wheat, Fruit and Nut Dessert

*1 Shredded Wheat*
*4 fl oz (115ml) unsweetened fruit juice*
*1 oz (30g) whole fruit jam*
*½ oz (15g) hazelnuts, toasted and*
  *chopped*

Heat gently all the ingredients together, turning the Shredded Wheat over to completely soften. Leave to cool in the serving bowl.

## 8. Pear and Carob Cream

*1 pear, cored and halved*
*2 oz (55g) curd cheese*
*1 oz (15g) natural yogurt*
*1 teaspoon carob powder*
*1 oz (30g) raisins*

Liquidize half the pear, curd cheese, yogurt and carob powder. Add the rest of the pear, chopped, and the raisins. Chill.

**250 cals**
**approximately**

## 7. Fried Bananas in Brandy

*1 banana, sliced*
*½ oz (15g) vegetable margarine*
*1 fl oz (30ml) brandy*

Fry the banana slices in the margarine until they are just tender. Serve with warmed brandy poured over the top.

## 8. Apple, Raisin and Nut Dessert

*1 apple, grated*
*½ oz (15g) nuts, finely chopped*
*1½ oz (45g) raisins*
*½ small carton natural yogurt*

Mix the fruit and nuts together, add a little lemon juice and cinnamon and soak overnight. Stir half the mixture into the yogurt and serve topped with the rest.

# 3.
# DAY PLANS

## Sample Daily Menus

The following suggested meals for a whole day may be helpful when you are working out the calories and content of your daily diet plan.

Try to ensure that your day's meals do not rely too heavily on dairy produce and that you get a significant amount of your protein from vegetable sources.

In the next section, 'Your Own Menus', there is a seven day menu plan for you to fill in. Once you have a record of seven day plans then you have your diet for a week easily available.

## The 1,000 Calorie Day

The ½ pint (285ml) skimmed/soy milk to be used in tea or coffee throughout the day, or just to drink when you like.

| | |
|---|---|
| Breakfast: (page 14) | Toast with Yogurt Fruit Drink and ½ oz (15g) low fat spread (from daily allowance) |
| Light/Easy Meal: (page 26) | Jacket Potato with Creamy Hazelnut Topping and remaining ½ oz (15g) low fat spread (from daily allowance) Mixed salad of 'free' vegetables |

| | |
|---|---|
| More Effort/ Family Meals: (page 66) | Spinach Roulade with Creamed Carrot and Swede (¼ portion) |
| Dessert: (page 42) | Banana with Blackcurrant |

## The 1,300 Calorie Day

Use the 7 oz (200g) natural yogurt and 1 orange peeled and chopped, both from the daily allowance, to make a dessert or snack to be eaten when you like during the the day.

| | |
|---|---|
| Breakfast: (page 17) | Nutty Cereal |
| Light/Easy Meal: (page 31) | Crispy Cheese Topped Vegetables, e.g. courgettes Simple salad of 'free' vegetables and 1 apple |
| More Effort/ Family Meals: (page 76) | Lentil and Millet Squares with Tomato Sauce (¼ portion) Steamed broccoli with ½ oz (15g) vegetable margarine (from daily allowance) melted over |
| Dessert: (page 38) | Apricot and Pineapple Crumble |

— 45 —

## The Vegan 1,300 Calorie Day

Liquidize the ½ pint (285ml) soy milk and 1 banana, both from the daily allowance, to make a drink for any time during the day.

Breakfast: (page 15) — Bread or Toast with Nut Butter

Light/Easy Meal: (page 21) — Chick-pea-and-mushroom-filled Pitta Bread and 1 oz (30g) low fat spread (from daily allowance)
Mixed salad of 'free' vegetables

More Effort/ Family Meals: (page 78) — Bean and Rice Stuffed Marrow with Sesame Parsnips (¼ portion)

Dessert: (page 40) — Hazelnut and Fruit Dessert

## The 'No Time To Cook' 1,300 Calorie Day

The ½ pint (285ml) skimmed/soy milk to be used in tea or coffee throughout the day or just drink it when you like.

Breakfast: (page 17) — Shredded Wheat and Yogurt

Light/Easy Meal: (page 21) — Nut Butter and Banana Sandwich
Mixed Salad of 'free' vegetables

More Effort/ Family Meals: (pages 87 and 70) — Stuffed Pepper
Green salad of 'free' vegetables

Dessert: (page 38) — Apricot Fool

Evening Snack: — 2 wholemeal crispbreads with ½ oz (15g) vegetable margarine (from daily allowance)
1 apple (from daily allowance)

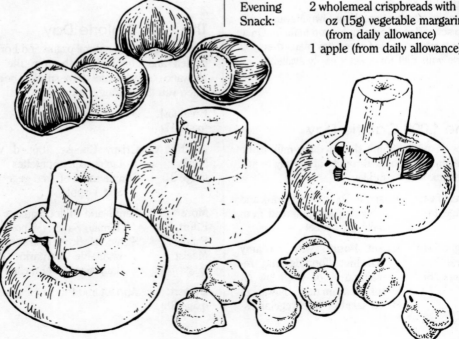

## The Nibbler's 1,300 Calorie Day

The ½ pint (285ml) skimmed/soy milk to be used in tea or coffee throughout the day.

| | |
|---|---|
| Early Morning Snack: | 1 wholemeal biscuit |
| Breakfast: (page 18) | Bean Fritters |
| Midmorning Snack: | 1 small wholemeal roll with ½ oz (15g) vegetable margarine (from daily allowance) |
| Light/Easy Meal: (page 28) | Broccoli with Cottage Cheese Grilled tomatoes |
| Afternoon Snack: (page 41) | Marzipan Filled Fruit |
| More Effort/ Family Meals: (page 71) | Red Kidney Bean and Walnut Roast (¼ portion) Mixed salad of 'free' vegetables |
| Evening Snack: | 1 apple (from daily allowance) |

## The 'Going To Town' 1,500 Calorie Day

The ½ pint (285ml) skimmed/soy milk to be used in tea or coffee throughout the day.

| | |
|---|---|
| Breakfast: (page 19) | Cheese Whirls with Tomatoes and Roll with 1 oz (30g) low fat spread (from daily allowance) |
| Lunch (page 86) | Rice Stuffed Cabbage Leaves Baked in Coconut Sauce with Fried Tofu (¼ portion) Mixed salad of 'free' vegetables |
| Dessert: (page 36) | Mango and Cardamom Cream |
| Evening Meal: (soup, see page 56) (flan, see page 72) | Tomato and Basil Soup Spiced Lentil Flan (⅙ portion) Lightly cooked 'free' vegetables 1 orange |
| Late Snack: | Crudités of sliced 'free' vegetables, e.g., carrot, cucumber celery, etc. and 1 apple (from daily allowance) |

# Simply Slim

# Your Own Menus

## Day 1: Calorie Total _____

| Recipe page number | Meal | Cals |
|---|---|---|
| | **Breakfast** | |
| | **Midmorning Snack** | |
| | **Midday Meal** | |
| | **Dessert** | |
| | **Afternoon Snack** | |
| | **Evening Meal** | |
| | **Late Snack** | |
| | **Notes** | |

## Day 2: Calorie Total _____

| Recipe page number | Meal | Cals |
|---|---|---|
| | Breakfast | |
| | Midmorning Snack | |
| | Midday Meal | |
| | Dessert | |
| | Afternoon Snack | |
| | Evening Meal | |
| | Late Snack | |
| | Notes | |

## Day 3: Calorie Total _____

| Recipe page number | Meal | Cals |
|---|---|---|
| | Breakfast | |
| | Midmorning Snack | |
| | Midday Meal | |
| | Dessert | |
| | Afternoon Snack | |
| | Evening Meal | |
| | Late Snack | |
| | Notes | |

Day 4: Calorie Total _____

| Recipe Page Number | Meal | Cals |
|---|---|---|
| | Breakfast | |
| | Midmorning Snack | |
| | Midday Meal | |
| | Dessert | |
| | Afternoon Snack | |
| | Evening Meal | |
| | Late Snack | |
| | Notes | |

# Simply Slim

## Day 5: Calorie Total _____

| Recipe page number | Meal | Cals |
|---|---|---|
| | Breakfast | |
| | Midmorning Snack | |
| | Midday Meal | |
| | Dessert | |
| | Afternoon Snack | |
| | Evening Meal | |
| | Late Snack | |
| | Notes | |

Day 6: Calorie Total _____

| Recipe Page Number | Meal | Cals |
|---|---|---|
| | Breakfast | |
| | Midmorning Snack | |
| | Midday Meal | |
| | Dessert | |
| | Afternoon Snack | |
| | Evening Meal | |
| | Late Snack | |
| | Notes | |

## Day 7: Calorie Total _____

| Recipe page number | Meal | Cals |
|---|---|---|
| | Breakfast | |
| | Midmorning Snack | |
| | Midday Meal | |
| | Dessert | |
| | Afternoon Snack | |
| | Evening Meal | |
| | Late Snack | |
| | Notes | |

## 4.

# RECIPES NOT JUST FOR ONE

## 'ree' Soups

free', low calorie vegetables are used to make ups then these can be included in the day's enu without allowing for them in the calorie :al, provided that only moderate quantities are :en.

Although suggested ingredients are given low, you can make up your own soups using out 1 lb (455g) vegetables to 1½ pints (850ml) getable stock and adding herbs or spices and asoning. Extra liquid or milk or yogurt from ur daily allowance will help to achieve the right nsistency.

The basic method for making a soup is to epare and chop the vegetables as necessary d simmer with the stock, herbs and seasoning r about 30 minutes. Liquidize all or some of e soup depending on the texture you want. If you want to add counting ingredients—such potatoes, lentils, rice or beans — you must member to check that you have sufficient are calories in your daily total.

## Suggested 'Free' Soup Ingredients

(Use the basic method described above)

## Courgette and Watercress Soup

*1 lb (455g) courgettes, trimmed and sliced*
*½ bunch watercress, chopped*
*1½ pints (850ml) vegetable stock*
*Seasoning*

## Celeriac and Watercress Soup

*2 bunches watercress, chopped*
*8 oz (225g) celeriac, diced*
*1 onion, chopped*
*1½ pints (850ml) vegetable stock*
*Seasoning*

# Jerusalem Artichoke Soup

*1½ lb (680g) Jerusalem artichokes, peeled or
    scraped and sliced
1 onion, chopped
1½ pints (850ml) vegetable stock
Seasoning
Pinch nutmeg*
*Squeeze lemon juice* } *add just before serving*

# Tomato and Basil Soup

*2 lb (900g) ripe tomatoes, chopped
Spring onions, chopped
1 small red pepper, deseeded and chopped
¾ pint (425ml) vegetable stock
Few drops Tabasco sauce
Dash dry white wine
2 tablespoons fresh chopped or 2 teaspoons dry
    basil
Seasoning*

# Spinach and Nutmeg Soup

*1 lb (455g) fresh spinach, chopped
Spring onions, chopped
1 pint (570ml) vegetable stock
Seasoning
Nutmeg, to garnish*

# Curried Parsnip Soup

*1½ lb (680g) parsnips, chopped
2 onions, chopped
1½ pints (850ml) vegetable stock
1 heaped teaspoon curry powder
Seasoning*

# Green Vegetable Soup

*8 oz (225g) French or runner beans, sliced
2 bunches watercress, chopped
2 leeks, sliced
8 oz (225g) fresh spinach, chopped
4 celery sticks, with leaves, chopped
1½ pints (850ml) vegetable stock
Seasoning*

# Mushroom Soup

*1 lb (455g) mushrooms, chopped
1 onion, chopped
1 tablespoon soy sauce
1 bay leaf (remove before liquidizing)
1½ pints (850ml) vegetable stock
Seasoning*

# Carrot and Coriander Soup

*1 lb (455g) carrots, sliced
1 large onion, chopped
1½ pints (850ml) vegetable stock
Seasoning
1 tablespoon lemon juice*
*Chopped fresh coriander* } *add at the end*

# Carrot and Orange Soup

*1 lb (455g) carrots, sliced
1 large onion, chopped
Rind of 1 orange
1½ pints (850ml) vegetable stock
Seasoning
Juice ½ orange*
*Fresh parsley, chopped* } *add at the end*

## ree' Salads

ing the full variety of 'free' low calorie
getables, it is easy to make many different
ads that do not have to be allowed for in the
ly calorie total if only moderate portions are
en.

Below are some suggested combinations for
'e' salads and all that you need do is simply
op, slice or grate the vegetables as necessary.
mon juice, herbs, spices and seasoning can
used liberally, and yogurt from your daily
owance (or as an extra, adding on calories to
ir daily total) can be used to make a salad
essing.

ngredients with significant calorific values,
ch as fruit, sweet corn, peas, beans, potatoes,
lses and nuts, can be included in the salad,
ovided that their calories do not exceed your
ily total.

## reen Salads

ung spinach leaves + leeks + celeriac +
spring onion

itercress + cauliflower (cooked) + young
turnips + green pepper

ttuce + fennel + spring onions + cucumber
+ mustard and cress

occoli (cooked) + celery + parsley + spring
onions (+ nutmeg)

urgettes + fennel + French beans (cooked)
+ onion + parsley

## Mixed Salads

Aubergines, peppers, onions (cooked together)
+ tomatoes (+ turmeric)

Tomatoes + fennel + watercress + spring
onion + orange rind

Broccoli (cooked) + tomatoes + onion +
mushrooms (+ lovage or rosemary)

Leeks + tomato + cucumber + bean sprouts
+ onion + peppers

Cauliflower (cooked) + French beans (cooked)
+ red peppers + onion (+ dill weed)

Lettuce + courgettes + radishes + spring
onion + tomatoes + carrot

## Crunchy Salads

Celeriac + lentil sprouts + peppers + carrot
+ tomatoes (+ cumin powder)

Red cabbage + parsnips + onion + mustard
and cress + lemon rind

Chicory + tomatoes + celery + peppers +
onion + bean shoots (+ mint)

White cabbage + carrot + onion + celery +
peppers + parsley

Beetroot + onion + carrot + peppers +
mustard and cress

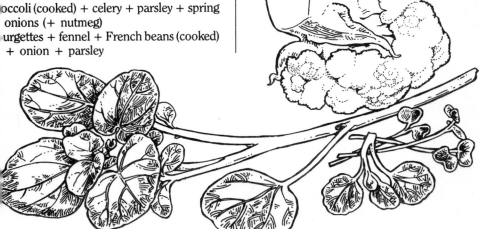

# Simply Slim

## More Effort/Family Meals — Index

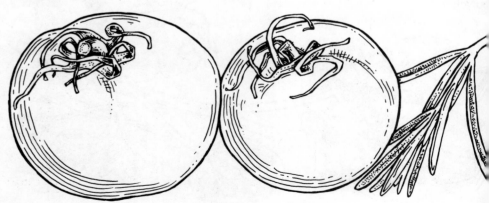

## More Effort/Family Meals

The following recipes should serve four people, unless stated otherwise, and are grouped according to the number of calories per portion, starting with the lower calorie recipes.

*Note*: Where no quantities are given for such ingredients as 'free' vegetables this is so you can use what you have to hand, or prefer, and to add variety. These ingredients also, in moderate quantities, add few or no calories to your diet (see also 'Free' vegetables, page 11).

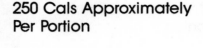

## 250 Cals Approximately Per Portion

## Tofu and Vegetable Slices

### Ingredients

*2 onions, finely chopped*
*2 red peppers, finely chopped*
*2 sticks celery, finely chopped*
*4 tablespoons soy sauce*
*8 oz (225g) tinned or cooked sweet corn*
*4 oz (115g) rolled oats*
*10 oz (285g) silken tofu, mashed*
*2 tablespoons fresh chopped or 2 teaspoons dried marjoram*
*Seasoning*
*A handful of sesame seeds, for garnishing*

### Method

1. Sauté the onions, peppers and celery in the soy sauce for about 5 minutes.
2. Remove from the heat and add the remaining ingredients, mixing well.
3. Press into a shallow tin, sprinkle over a few sesame seeds and put under a medium hot grill for about 15 minutes until brown and firm.
4. Cut into slices to serve.

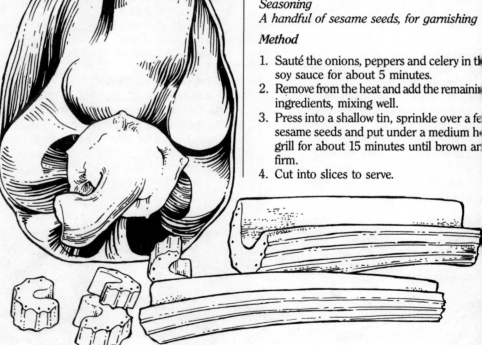

# Spinach and Cheese Fritters

*Ingredients*

1 lb (455g) fresh or 8 oz (225g) frozen
  spinach, cooked and chopped
8 oz (225g) fresh wholemeal breadcrumbs
6 oz (170g) cottage cheese
2 oz (55g) medium fat cheese, grated
Spring onions, chopped
2 tablespoons fresh parsley, chopped
2 teaspoons dried basil
2 eggs, beaten
Seasoning

*Method*

Mix all of the ingredients together well.
Form into fairly flat rounds and fry on both
sides until crisp.

# Potato and Mushroom Cutlets

*Ingredients*

8 oz (225g) mushrooms, finely chopped
2 onions, finely chopped
2 teaspoons yeast extract
1½ lb (680g) cooked potatoes, mashed
3 oz (85g) medium fat cheese, grated
1 oz (30g) fresh wholemeal breadcrumbs
1 teaspoon dried mixed herbs
Seasoning

*Method*

Sauté the mushrooms and onions in the yeast
extract for about 5 minutes.
Drain off any surplus liquid from the
mushrooms before mixing them well with the
other ingredients.
Form into firm cutlets and fry or grill on both
sides.

# Cheese-stuffed Courgettes

*Ingredients*

1 lb (455g) courgettes
4 oz (115g) curd cheese
2 oz (55g) medium fat cheese, grated
2 oz (55g) walnuts, chopped
Spring onions or chives, chopped
3 eggs, separated
Seasoning

*Method*

1. Cut the courgettes in half lengthways and
   scoop out the pith to form boat shapes out
   of the skins (keep the pith for soups, burgers
   or bakes).
2. Mash the curd cheese with the grated cheese,
   walnuts, beaten egg yolks and seasoning.
3. Fold the stiffly beaten egg whites into the
   cheese mixture and pile into the courgette
   halves.
4. Bake at Gas Mark 6, 200°C or 400°F for
   25-30 minutes.

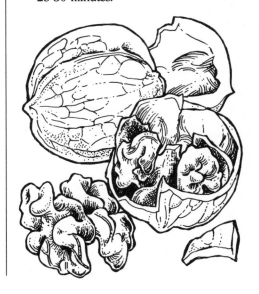

# Potato-stuffed Mushrooms with Spiced Vegetables and Beans

*Ingredients for Potato-stuffed Mushrooms*

1 onion, finely chopped
1 tablespoon vegetable oil
½ inch (1.25cm) root ginger, grated
1 garlic clove, crushed
8 oz (225g) cooked potato, mashed
Seasoning
1 tablespoon lemon juice
1 tablespoon fresh coriander or parsley,
    chopped
20 large button mushrooms
4 oz (115g) medium fat cheese, grated

*Method for Potato-stuffed Mushrooms*

1. Fry the onion in the oil for a few minutes. Then add the ginger and garlic and fry for a few more minutes.
2. Mix the onion mixture and mashed potato together, season and add the lemon juice and herbs.
3. Remove the stalks from the mushrooms (saving them to use in the Spiced Vegetables and Beans recipe below) and fill the hollows with the onion and potato mixture. Sprinkle the grated cheese on top.
4. Bake the filled mushrooms at Gas Mark 5, 190°C or 375°F for 10-15 minutes.

*Ingredients for Spiced Vegetables and Beans*

'Free' vegetables of your choice
Mushroom stalks (from above)
8 oz (225g) cooked or tinned beans
2-3 teaspoons garam masala or curry
    powder

*Method for Spiced Vegetables and Beans*

1. Sauté the vegetables and mushroom stalks in a covered pan with the beans and garam masala or curry powder until the vegetable are tender. Add a little water or vegetabl stock if necessary.

# Mushroom-stuffed Aubergines with Cottage Cheese Salac

*Ingredients for Mushroom-stuffed Aubergine*

4 medium aubergines
2 large onions, finely chopped
12 oz (340g) button mushrooms
8 large tomatoes, skinned and chopped
4 oz (115g) fresh wholemeal breadcrumbs
2 lemons, squeezed, peel finely chopped
2 teaspoons dried marjoram
Seasoning
2 eggs, beaten

*Method for Mushroom-stuffed Aubergines*

1. Boil the aubergines whole for 2 minutes. Cu in half lengthways, and remove the flesh carefully and chop.
2. Sauté the aubergine flesh, onions mushrooms and tomatoes until the onion i just tender.
3. Remove from the heat, add the breadcrumbs juice and peel of the lemon, herbs and seasoning, finally binding with the beater egg.
4. Fill the aubergine halves and bake covered for about 45 minutes at Gas Mark 4, 180°C or 350°F.

*Ingredients for Cottage Cheese Salad*

8 oz (225g) cottage cheese
Mix of 'free' vegetables

*Method for Cottage Cheese Salad*

1. Either mix the cottage cheese with your salad or spoon it on top as a garnish.

# occoli Bake with range and Nut Celery

*redients for Broccoli Bake*

*ggs, separated*
*z (115g) curd cheese*
*z (115g) cottage cheese*
*ch mace or nutmeg*
*soning*
*b (455g) broccoli, cooked and chopped or mashed*
*ing onions, chopped*

*thod for Broccoli Bake*

Beat the egg yolks into the cheeses and add the spice and seasoning.
Add the broccoli and spring onion to the cheese mixture.
Fold in the stiffly beaten egg whites, spoon the mixture into a dish or tin and bake at Gas Mark 4, 180°C or 350°F for about 30 minutes, or until risen.

*redients for Orange and Nut Celery*

*mall heads celery*
*ranges*
*z (55g) walnuts, chopped*
*soning*

*thod for Orange and Nut Celery*

Cut each celery stick into 1½-2 inch (3.75-5cm) lengths.
Grate the peel from one of the oranges and squeeze the juice from both.
Put the celery, walnuts and orange peel into a dish, pour the orange juice over and sprinkle with any seasoning you may want to add.
Cover and cook for about 30 minutes at Gas Mark 4, 180°C or 350°F, or until the celery is tender.

# Savoury Egg and Rice Loaf with Braised Cabbage

## Ingredients for Savoury Egg and Rice Loaf

4 oz (115g) brown rice, cooked
4 oz (115g) fresh or frozen peas, cooked
4 oz (115g) button mushrooms, chopped
1 large onion, finely chopped
1 tablespoon tomato purée
1 tablespoon soy sauce
½ teaspoon allspice powder
Seasoning
2 eggs, beaten
2 eggs, hard-boiled

## Method for Savoury Egg and Rice Loaf

1. Mix together all of the ingredients except for the hard-boiled eggs.
2. Spoon half of the mixture into a 1 lb (455g) loaf tin and place the two hard-boiled eggs lengthways on top.
3. Pack the rest of the rice mixture around and on top of the eggs and cover with greaseproof paper.
4. Bake at Gas Mark 4, 180°C or 350°F for 40-45 minutes.

## Ingredients for Braised Cabbage

2 onions, sliced
1½ lb (680g) firm green cabbage, shredded
½ teaspoon nutmeg
Seasoning

## Method for Braised Cabbage

1. Place the onions, cabbage, nutmeg and seasoning in a pan with a little water and cook covered over a gentle heat for about 20 minutes, or until the vegetables are just tender.
2. Serve with chopped tomato, chives or parsley on top.

## Carrot and Watercress Loaf with Creamy Mushrooms

*Ingredients for Carrot and Watercress Loaf*

*1 large tomato, sliced*
*10 oz (285g) potatoes, diced*
*2 bunches watercress, chopped*
*Spring onions, chopped*
*1 tablespoon fresh parsley, chopped*
*2 oz (55g) medium fat cheese, grated*
*Seasoning*
*8 oz (225g) carrots, cooked*
*4 oz (115g) cooked butter beans or 1 15 oz*
*   (425g) tin, drained*
*1 onion, finely chopped*
*2 teaspoons caraway seeds (optional)*
*¼ teaspoon nutmeg*
*Seasoning*

*Method for Carrot and Watercress Loaf*

1. Arrange the tomato slices on the bottom of a 2 lb (900g) non-stick loaf tin.
2. Cook the potatoes, adding the watercress towards the end of their cooking time, drain and purée.
3. Add the spring onions, parsley and cheese to the potato mixture, and season.
4. Purée the carrots, beans and onion, stir in the spices and seasoning and pack into the tin.
5. Pile the potato and watercress mixture on top of the carrot purée and bake at Gas Mark 5, 190°C or 375°F for about 25 minutes. Serve hot or cold.

*Ingredients for Creamy Mushrooms*

*1 lb (455g) button mushrooms sliced or*
*   chopped*
*1 tablespoon soy sauce*
*¼ teaspoon dried marjoram or basil*
*1 small carton natural yogurt*

*Method for Creamy Mushrooms*

1. Sauté the mushrooms with the soy sauce a marjoram or basil until tender.
2. Let cool a little and stir in the yogurt, gen warming through.

## Celeriac-filled Buckwheat Pancakes

*Ingredients*

*2 oz (55g) wholemeal flour*
*2 oz (55g) buckwheat flour*
*1 egg, beaten*
*½ pint (285ml) skimmed milk*
*1½ lb (680g) celeriac, diced*
*8 oz (225g) leeks, sliced*
*4 oz (115g) fresh or frozen peas*
*3 oz (85g) medium fat cheese, grated*
*1 tablespoon fresh herbs (e.g. lovage,*
*   parsley, thyme), chopped*
*Seasoning*

*Method*

1. Make a batter with the flours, egg and m and leave to stand while following step
2. Meanwhile, lightly cook (boil, sauté, stir- or steam) the celeriac, leeks, peas and a the cheese, herbs and seasoning and ke warm.
3. Make 8-10 pancakes with the batter a divide the filling between them. Roll the up and place in a hot oven or under the g to heat through.

# Cauliflower-filled Yogurt Pancakes with Cumin Courgettes

*Ingredients for Cauliflower-filled Yogurt Pancakes*

4 oz (115g) wholemeal flour
1 egg, beaten
1 small carton natural yogurt
1 teaspoon coriander powder
½ oz (15g) dessicated coconut
1 tablespoon fresh coriander or parsley, chopped
Seasoning
1 small cauliflower, chopped
1 onion, finely chopped
2 tomatoes, skinned and chopped
½ inch (1.25cm) root ginger, grated
1 tablespoon soy sauce
Seasoning
Juice of ½ lemon
4 oz (115g) quark or other low fat cheese

*Method for Cauliflower-filled Yogurt Pancakes*

1. Make a batter with the flour, egg and the yogurt, made up to ½ pint (285ml) with water. Add more water if necessary to make a batter of pouring consistency.
2. Add the coriander powder, coconut, fresh coriander or parsley and seasoning. Mix well and leave to stand whilst making the filling.
3. Place the cauliflower, onion, tomatoes and ginger with the soy sauce and seasoning in a shallow pan, cover and cook gently until the vegetables are tender, giving the pan an occasional shake.
4. Stir in the quark or other low fat cheese, warm through and keep hot.
5. Make 8-10 pancakes with the batter, divide the filling between them and roll up, finally placing them in a hot oven or under the grill to heat through.

*Ingredients for Cumin Courgettes*

1 lb (455g) courgettes, sliced
1 onion, finely chopped
1 garlic clove, crushed
1 teaspoon cumin powder
Seasoning

*Method for Cumin Courgettes*

1. Place the courgettes, onion, garlic, cumin powder and seasoning in a shallow pan with a little water.
2. Cover and steam over a gentle heat until the vegetables are just tender.

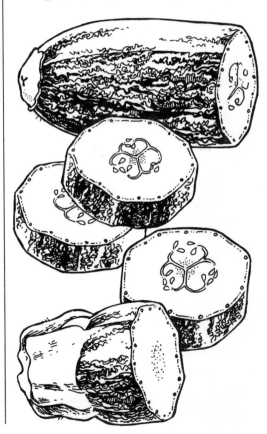

# Vegetable-filled Pancakes with Rosemary Tomatoes

*Ingredients for Vegetable-filled Pancakes*

4 oz (115g) wholemeal flour
1 egg, beaten
½ pint (285ml) skimmed milk
8 oz (225g) bean shoots
1 onion, finely chopped
4 oz (115g) fresh or frozen peas
4 oz (115g) waterchestnuts, chopped
1 tablespoon soy sauce
4 oz (115g) pineapple, fresh or canned,
    drained from natural juice
8 oz (115g) cottage cheese
Paprika

*Method for Vegetable-filled Pancakes*

1. Make a batter with the flour, egg and milk, then leave to stand while following step 2.
2. Stir-fry the vegetables in the soy sauce until they are tender and add the pineapple to heat through.
3. Make 8-10 small pancakes, divide the filling between them and roll up.
4. Arrange in a shallow dish, top with cottage cheese and a sprinkle of paprika and place under a hot grill to brown the top.

*Ingredients for Rosemary Tomatoes*

1 lb (455g) tomatoes, quartered
1 tablespoon fresh chopped or 1 teaspoon
    dried rosemary
Lemon juice
Black pepper

*Method for Rosemary Tomatoes*

1. Place the tomatoes, rosemary and a squeeze of lemon juice in a pan, stir well, cover and steam over a gentle heat so that the tomatoes are cooked a little but still intact.
2. Sprinkle with black pepper and serve.

# Spinach Roulade with Creamed Carrot and Swede

*Ingredients for Spinach Roulade*

1 lb (455g) fresh spinach or 8 oz (225g)
    frozen, lightly cooked, drained well and
    chopped
4 eggs, separated
1 teaspoon vegetable oil
8 oz (225g) button mushrooms, chopped
1 teaspoon yeast extract
½ oz (15g) wholemeal flour
¼ pint (140ml) skimmed milk
4 oz (115g) quark or other low fat cheese
Seasoning

*Method for Spinach Roulade*

1. Cool the spinach and stir in the beaten egg yolks.
2. Season and then fold in the stiffly beaten egg whites.
3. Lightly oil some greaseproof paper to line a Swiss roll tin and spread the spinach mixture over, baking at Gas Mark 7, 220°C or 425F° for 15 minutes.
4. Meanwhile make the filling by lightly frying the mushrooms in the yeast extract for 10 minutes.
5. Make a paste by mixing the flour with a little of the cold milk. Heat the rest of the milk and stir into the paste.
6. Return the milk and flour mixture to the heat and gently cook, stirring as it thickens.
7. Add the mushrooms, quark and seasoning to the sauce, and spread over the cooked roulade.
8. Roll up, as you would a Swiss roll, and return to the oven for 5 minutes.

*Ingredients for Creamed Carrot and Swede*

*1 lb (455g) swede, cooked*
*8 oz (225g) carrot, cooked*
*1 teaspoon dried thyme*
*Seasoning*
*8 oz (225g) tomatoes, sliced*
*1 oz (30g) fresh wholemeal breadcrumbs*
*½ oz (15g) vegetable oil*

*Method for Creamed Carrot and Swede*

1. Mash the swede and carrot together and add herbs and seasoning.
2. Spoon the mixture into a casserole dish, top with the sliced tomato, mix the breadcrumbs with the oil and put this on the top.
3. Place under a hot grill to brown and crisp the top.

# Curried Vegetables and Lentils

*Ingredients*

*1 oz (30g) creamed or dessicated coconut*
*8 oz (225g) continental lentils, soaked and drained*
*2 onions, chopped*
*1 bay leaf*
*1 whole fresh green chilli*
*1-inch (2.5cm) root ginger, grated*
*1 tablespoon turmeric*
*2 teaspoons each cumin and coriander powder*
*1½ lb (680g) 'free' vegetables, lightly cooked*
*3 teaspoons garam masala*
*Seasoning*

*Method*

1. Make some coconut milk by pouring ½ pint (285ml) boiling water over the coconut.
2. Place the lentils in a pan with water sufficient to cover, together with the onions, bay leaf, chilli, ginger, turmeric, cumin and coriander and simmer for about 20 minutes or until the lentils are tender.
3. Remove the bay leaf and chilli, stir in the vegetables, coconut milk and garam masala, season to taste and heat through.

# Chick-pea Casserole

*Ingredients*

*8 oz (225g) chick-peas, soaked and cooked or 2 15 oz (425g) tins, drained*
*2 lb (900g) tomatoes, skinned and chopped or 2 15 oz (425g) tins of tomatoes*
*8 oz (225g) cabbage, coarsely shredded*
*1 onion, finely chopped*
*2 oz (55g) raisins*
*1 teaspoon ground ginger*
*4 whole cloves*
*Seasoning*
*1 egg, hard-boiled*
*Fresh parsley, chopped, to garnish*

*Method*

1. Place all the ingredients except for the egg and parsley into a large pan and simmer for about 30 minutes.
2. Serve garnished with chopped egg and parsley.

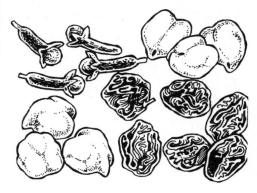

300 Calories Approximately
Per Portion

## Soya Bean and Hazelnut Fritters

### Ingredients

6 oz (170g) soya beans, cooked
4 oz (115g) hazelnuts, ground
4 oz (115g) button mushrooms, chopped
1 onion, finely chopped
1 egg, beaten
1 tablespoon tomato purée
1 teaspoon dried mixed herbs
Seasoning

### Method

1. Mash the beans well and mix with the remaining ingredients.
2. Form into thin patties and fry on both sides.

# Cauliflower and Almond Burgers with Corn and Peas

### Ingredients for Cauliflower and Almond Burgers

1 small cauliflower, cooked and mashed
4 oz (115g) almonds, ground
4 oz (115g) fresh wholemeal breadcrumbs
1 onion, finely chopped
1 tablespoon fresh or 1 teaspoon dried rosemary
Seasoning

### Method for Cauliflower and Almond Burger

1. Mix all ingredients together well.
2. Form into firm patties and place under a ho grill, turning to brown both sides.

### Ingredients for Corn and Peas

8 oz (225g) fresh or frozen peas
4 oz (115g) frozen or tinned sweet corn
'Free' vegetables of your choice (e.g. onions, tomatoes)
Herbs (such as mint)
Seasoning

### Method for Corn and Peas

1. Simmer the peas and sweet corn in a pa along with the 'free' vegetables and add herb and seasoning.

## Watercress and Potato Burgers

### Ingredients

1 lb (455g) cooked potatoes, mashed
1 bunch watercress, finely chopped
4 oz (115g) fresh or frozen peas, cooked
4 oz (115g) walnuts, ground
4 oz (115g) tofu, mashed
Spring onions, chopped
1 tablespoon fresh mint chopped or 1
  teaspoon dried mint
Seasoning

### Method

Mix all the ingredients together well.
Form into burgers and fry on both sides.

## Nutty Stuffed Tomatoes with Pepper Sauce and Bean Salad

### Ingredients for Nutty Stuffed Tomatoes

4 large tomatoes
8 oz (225g) cottage cheese
4 oz (115g) nuts, ground
2 sticks of celery, finely chopped
2 spring onions, chopped
1 teaspoon dried basil
Seasoning

### Method for Nutty Stuffed Tomatoes

Cut the tops off the tomatoes and carefully
remove the centre pulp.
Mix all the filling ingredients together, stuff
the tomatoes with the mixture and replace
the tops.
Bake them at Gas Mark 5, 190°C or 375°F
for 20 minutes.

### Ingredients for Pepper Sauce

3 green peppers
2 garlic cloves, crushed
Juice of ½ lemon
Seasoning

### Method for Pepper Sauce

1. Simmer the peppers whole with the garlic
   in water for about 10 minutes.
2. Drain, reserving about 2 fl oz (60ml) of the
   liquid.
3. Purée the peppers with the lemon juice and
   sufficient cooking liquid to achieve your
   preferred consistency. Season to taste.
4. Serve sauce either hot with the Stuffed
   Tomatoes or cold with the Bean Salad.

### Ingredients for Bean Salad

'Free' vegetables of your choice
6 oz (170g) cooked or tinned beans

### Method for Bean Salad

1. Mix all the vegetables together and serve.

# Cheese-and-apple-stuffed Peppers with Tomato and Egg Scramble

*Ingredients for Cheese-and-apple-stuffed Peppers*

4 peppers
4 oz (115g) fresh wholemeal breadcrumbs
4 oz (115g) medium fat cheese, grated
1 apple, grated
1 oz (30g) walnuts, chopped
Spring onions, chopped
1 teaspoon dried rosemary
Seasoning
1 egg, beaten

*Method for Cheese-and-apple-stuffed Peppers*

1. Boil the peppers for a few minutes, cut off the tops and reserve, but discard the pith and seeds.
2. Mix all of the filling ingredients together adding sufficient beaten egg to make a firm mixture.
3. Fill the peppers, replace the tops and bake covered at Gas Mark 6, 200°C or 400°F for about 30 minutes.

*Ingredients for Tomato and Egg Scramble*

3 eggs, beaten
Tomato, finely chopped
Spring onion, chopped
Parsley, chopped
Seasoning

*Method for Tomato and Egg Scramble*

1. Mix together all the ingredients.
2. Stir in a shallow pan over a moderate heat until the eggs set.

# Cheese-and-nut-stuffed Onions with Minted Bean Ratatouille

*Ingredients for Cheese-and-nut-stuffed Onions*

4 large onions
4 oz (115g) medium fat cheese, grated
3 oz (85g) nuts, ground
2 oz (55g) fresh wholemeal breadcrumbs
1 tablespoon tomato purée
1 teaspoon dried oregano
Seasoning

*Method for Cheese-and-nut-stuffed Onions*

1. Peel the onions and cook whole in boiling water until they are just tender.
2. Cool the onions slightly, remove the centre carefully and finely chop them.
3. Mix the chopped onion with the remaining ingredients and fill the onion shells.
4. Bake the stuffed onions at Gas Mark 190°C or 375°F for 30 minutes.

*Ingredients for Minted Bean Ratatouille*

Peppers, sliced
Courgettes, sliced
Onions, sliced
Tomatoes, skinned and chopped
4 oz (115g) cooked or tinned beans
Fresh mint, chopped
Seasoning

*Method for Minted Bean Ratatouille*

1. Sauté all the ingredients in a covered pan until the vegetables are just tender.

## ed-kidney-bean-and-
## ʼalnut Roast

*ʼredients*

ʼz (115g) cooked red kidney beans or
1 15 oz (425g) tin, drained
ʼz (115g) walnuts, ground
ʼz (115g) tomatoes, skinned and chopped
ʼreen pepper, deseeded and chopped
ʼnion, finely chopped
ʼz (85g) fresh wholemeal breadcrumbs
ʼgg, beaten
ʼarlic clove, crushed (optional)
ʼeaspoon dried mixed herbs
ʼeaspoons garam masala
ʼasoning

*ʼthod*

Mix all ingredients together well and pile into
a 7 inch (18cm) square tin.
Bake at Gas Mark 5, 190°C or 375°F for 45
minutes.

# Gingered Lentil and Pineapple Loaf with Tofu-dressed Salad

*Ingredients for Gingered Lentil and Pineapple Loaf*

8 oz (225g) lentils, red or green
1 onion, chopped
12 fl oz (340ml) vegetable stock
2 teaspoons fresh grated or 1 teaspoon
    dried ginger
3 oz (85g) fresh wholemeal breadcrumbs
6 oz (170g) pineapple fresh or tinned,
    drained from natural juice, finely
    chopped
2 tablespoons fresh parsley, chopped
1 egg, beaten
Seasoning

*Method for Gingered Lentil and Pineapple Loaf*

1. Simmer the lentils, onions and ginger in the vegetable stock until the lentils are tender and the liquid has been absorbed.
2. Mix the lentils with the other ingredients and pile into a 2 lb (900g) loaf tin.
3. Bake at Gas Mark 5, 190°C or 375°F for 40 minutes.

*Ingredients for Tofu-dressed Salad*

'Free' vegetables of your choice
4 oz (115g) tofu
Lemon juice
Herbs
Seasoning

*Method for Tofu-dressed Salad*

1. Chop and mix together the 'free' vegetables.
2. Blend the tofu with the lemon juice, herbs and seasoning and pour over the salad.

## Vegetable and Oat Pie

*Ingredients*

*1 lb (455g) cabbage, sliced*
*8 oz (225g) carrots, sliced*
*2 onions, sliced*
*2 tablespoons soy sauce*
*1 teaspoon dried mixed herbs*
*4 oz (115g) rolled oats*
*2 oz (55g) fresh wholemeal breadcrumbs*
*4 oz (115g) cottage cheese*
*2 tomatoes, skinned and chopped*
*2 eggs, beaten*
*Seasoning*
*2 oz (55g) medium fat cheese, grated*

*Method*

1. In a covered pan sauté the vegetables in the soy sauce until tender.
2. Mix together the oats, breadcrumbs, cottage cheese, tomatoes, beaten eggs and seasoning.
3. Place the cooked vegetables in a casserole dish, top with the oat mixture and sprinkle the grated cheese over the top.
4. Bake at Gas Mark 6, 200°C or 400°F for 30 minutes.

## Spiced Lentil Flan (serves 6

*Ingredients*

*7 oz (200g) wholemeal flour*
*2½ oz (70g) vegetable margarine*
*3½ oz (100g) cooked potato, mashed*
*1 onion, chopped*
*4 oz (115g) red lentils*
*6 fl oz (170ml) vegetable stock*
*1 teaspoon cumin*
*1 bay leaf*
*1 tablespoon creamed coconut*
*Lemon juice*
*1 egg, beaten*
*1 small carton natural yogurt*
*1 tablespoon fresh coriander, chopped*
*Seasoning*
*Sesame seeds or dessicated coconut*

*Method*

1. Sift the flour and add back the bran, mix i the margarine to form crumbs and the knead in the mashed potato.
2. Add a little water if necessary to form a so dough and roll out between sheets polythene, remove the polythene and the line a flan tin.
3. Bake the pastry case blind at Gas Mark 200°C or 400°F for 10 minutes.
4. Simmer the onion and lentils in the stoc with the cumin and bay leaf until the liqui is absorbed and the lentils are cooked.
5. Stir the creamed coconut into the lentils, a a squeeze of lemon juice and spread th mixture into the cooked pastry case.
6. Beat together the egg and yogurt, add th coriander and seasoning and put this on to of the lentil mixture.
7. Sprinkle some sesame seeds or coconut ove the flan and return to the oven for about 2 minutes to set the egg mixture.

## Chick-pea Pancakes with Smoked Aubergine

*Ingredients for Chick-pea Pancakes*

*8 oz (225g) chick-pea flour (gram flour)*
*1 carrot, grated*
*1 courgette, grated*
*1 onion, finely chopped*
*2 tablespoons fresh coriander, chopped*
*Pinch chilli powder*
*Seasoning*

*Method for Chick-pea Pancakes*

Make a batter with the chick-pea flour and about 12 fl oz (340ml) water. It should be of a pouring consistency.
Add the vegetables, spices and seasoning and leave to stand for 5-10 minutes.
Make small pancakes, cooking both sides.

*Ingredients for Smoked Aubergine*

*2 small aubergines*
*1 small carton natural yogurt*
*2 oz (55g) tahini*
*Juice of ½ lemon*
*Seasoning*

*Method for Smoked Aubergine*

Smoke the aubergines over a gas flame or under the grill, turning to char and blacken all over while also cooking the inside.
Pick off the skin of the aubergines and purée the flesh with the yogurt, tahini, lemon juice and seasoning.
Either spread the aubergine mixture over the pancakes and garnish with chopped tomato, spring onion and parsley, or serve the pancakes separately, topped with tomato, spring onion and the Smoked Aubergine dish garnished with parsley.

## Quick Pan Pizza (serves 2)

*Ingredients*

*4 oz (115g) self-raising wholemeal flour*
*¼ teaspoon baking powder*
*Pinch salt*
*Pinch dry mustard*
*1 onion, chopped*
*8 oz (225g) tomatoes, skinned and chopped*
*   or 1 small tin of tomatoes*
*4 oz (115g) button mushrooms, chopped*
*1 teaspoon dried oregano*
*Seasoning*
*2 oz (55g) cottage cheese*
*1½ oz (45g) medium fat cheese, grated*

*Method*

1. Sift the flour, baking powder, salt and mustard together, add back the bran and gradually add sufficient water to form a firm dough.
2. Simmer the onion, tomatoes, mushrooms, oregano and seasoning for about 10 minutes to reduce the tomato juice.
3. Meanwhile, press the dough into a 7-inch (18cm) round and cook in a shallow pan for 5 minutes, then turn.
4. Spread the tomato topping over the base, cover with the two cheeses mixed together and cook the base for a further 5 minutes.
5. Place under a hot grill to brown and crisp the top.

# Spiced Lentils and Rice

### Ingredients

6 oz (170g) continental lentils
6 oz (170g) long grain brown rice
2 onions, thinly sliced
1¾ pints (995ml) vegetable stock
½ teaspoon each cumin and allspice
    powder
Seasoning
Lemon juice

### Method

1. Bring the lentils, rice, vegetable stock and spices to the boil in a large saucepan, reduce to simmer and cook covered for 35-40 minutes, until the rice and lentils are tender and much of the liquid has been absorbed.
2. Leave to stand for 5-10 minutes, then add the seasoning and a squeeze of lemon juice.
3. This dish is best served with a salad of 'free' vegetables which includes tomatoes, onions, peppers and fresh, chopped parsley or coriander.

# Butter Bean and Potato Goulash

### Ingredients

8 oz (225g) butter beans, cooked until just
    tender
8 oz (225g) potato, diced
8 oz (225g) carrots, diced
2 onions, sliced
2 green peppers, deseeded and sliced
1 garlic clove, crushed
1 28 oz (790g) tin of tomatoes
1 oz (30g) tomato purée
1 oz (30g) raisins
3 teaspoons paprika
Seasoning
1 small carton natural yogurt
Fresh parsley, chopped, to garnish

### Method

1. Place all of the ingredients, except for th yogurt and parsley, in a pan. Bring to the bo and simmer for about 25 minutes to coo the vegetables and reduce the liquid.
2. Cool slightly, stir in the yogurt, gently war through again and pile into a dish, garnishin with parsley.

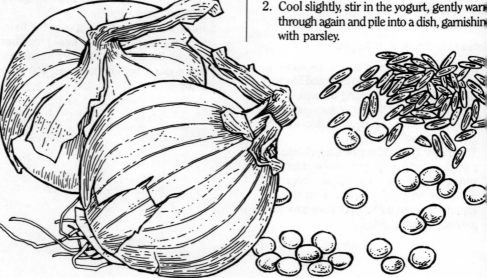

## Vegetable Moussaka with Citrus Parsnips

### Ingredients for Vegetable Moussaka

onions, chopped
carrots, sliced
sticks of celery, sliced
green pepper, deseeded and sliced
red pepper, deseeded and sliced
7 oz (200g) tin of tomatoes
large aubergine, diced
large courgette, sliced
oz (30g) tomato purée
teaspoon cinnamon powder
garlic clove, crushed
seasoning
½ oz (45g) wholemeal flour
fl oz (200ml) skimmed milk
teaspoon nutmeg
egg, beaten
oz (140g) cottage cheese, sieved or
  liquidized
oz (30g) medium fat cheese, grated

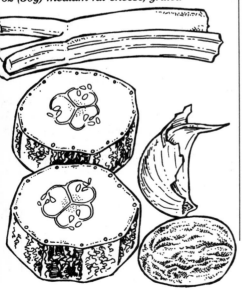

### Method for Vegetable Moussaka

1. Simmer the first twelve ingredients together in a covered pan for about 20 minutes, or until all the vegetables are just tender.
2. Make a paste with the flour and a little of the cold milk. Heat the rest of the milk and add gradually, stirring, to the paste.
3. Return the milk and flour mixture to the heat and cook, still stirring, until the sauce thickens. Then remove from the heat and cool slightly.
4. Add the nutmeg and a little of the cooled sauce to the beaten egg. Mix well and then add the egg mixture to the rest of the sauce.
5. Stir the cottage cheese into the sauce. Put the vegetables in a casserole dish, pour the sauce over them and top with the grated cheese.
6. Bake at Gas Mark 4, 180°C or 350°F for 45 minutes.

### Ingredients for Citrus Parsnips

1½ lb (680g) parsnips, cut into ½-inch
  (1.25cm) chunks
1 oz (30g) vegetable margarine
1 onion, finely chopped
Grated rind and juice of 1 lemon
Seasoning
Chopped chives or spring onion to garnish

### Method for Citrus Parsnips

1. Cook parsnips in boiling water for a few minutes and then drain.
2. Melt the margarine in a pan and fry the onion until soft.
3. Mix in the lemon juice and rind, the parsnips and seasoning.
4. Transfer parsnips to a baking tray and place under a hot grill, shaking occasionally, to crisp.

**400 Cals Approximately
Per Portion**

## Lentil and Millet Squares with Tomato Sauce

### Ingredients for Lentil and Millet Squares

*8 oz (225g) red lentils*
*8 oz (225g) millet*
*2 pints (1.1l) vegetable stock or water*
*1 onion, chopped*
*½ teaspoon ground cloves*
*2 tablespoons fresh parsley or coriander,
   chopped*
*1 teaspoon lemon juice*
*Seasoning*

### Method for Lentil and Millet Squares

1. Place lentils, millet, onion and clove powder
   in a pan with the stock and simmer, covered,
   until the lentils and millet are cooked and
   the liquid has been absorbed.
2. Add the herbs, lemon juice and seasoning,
   then press the mixture into a shallow tray and
   leave to cool.
3. Cut into squares and fry or grill on both sides.

### Ingredients for Tomato Sauce

*1 15 oz (425g) tin of tomatoes, chopped*
*1 onion, finely chopped*
*1 tablespoon tomato purée*
*1 teaspoon dried herbs*
*Seasoning*

### Method for Tomato Sauce

1. Simmer all ingredients together for about 20
   minutes to reduce the liquid.
2. Purée if you like a smooth consistency.

## Curried Cereal and Cheese Balls with Stir-fried Vegetables

### Ingredients for Curried Cereal and Cheese Balls

*8 oz (225g) brown rice or whole wheat or
   pot barley*
*8 oz (225g) medium fat cheese, grated*
*Spring onions, chopped*
*2 teaspoons curry powder*
*2 tablespoons fresh parsley or coriander,
   chopped*
*Seasoning*

### Method for Curried Cereal and Cheese Ba

1. Cook the cereal and drain off any surp
   liquid.
2. Mix all of the other ingredients in with t
   hot cereal and leave to cool.
3. Form into firm balls and fry them.

### Ingredients for Stir-fried Vegetables

*'Free' vegetables of your choice*
*Soy sauce*
*8 oz (225g) bamboo shoots, sliced*
*8 oz (225g) fresh or frozen peas*

### Method for Stir-fried Vegetables

1. Chop 'free' vegetables and stir-fry them w
   the sliced bamboo shoots and the peas
   the soy sauce over a high heat, stirri
   briskly.
2. When they are slightly crisp, serve at or
   with the Curried Cereal and Cheese Ba

## ʒiced Rice and ﾁa Burgers

*ʒredients*

*ɀ (225g) green split peas*
*ɀ (225g) brown rice*
*nions, finely chopped*
*nall oranges*
*int (570ml) vegetable stock or water*
*ʔaspoons coriander powder*
*ʔaspoon allspice powder*
*ʔsoning*

*ʔhod*

Cook the peas, rice, onion, orange rind and orange juice with the vegetable stock until both the peas and rice are tender and the liquid has been absorbed.
Leave to cool, mash and add the spices and seasoning.
Form into burgers and fry on both sides.

## ﾁubergine-stuffed ﾁmatoes with ﾁntils and Spinach

*ʔredients for Aubergine-stuffed Tomatoes*

*ʔubergines*
*ʔarlic cloves, crushed*
*ʔɀ (85g) tahini*
*ʔce of 2 lemons*
*ʔablespoons fresh parsley, chopped*
*ʔsoning*
*ʔrge tomatoes*

*ʔhod for Aubergine-stuffed Tomatoes*

Bake the aubergines whole at Gas Mark 3, 170°C or 325°F for about 30 minutes, or until soft.

2. Cool, cut in half, scoop out the pulp and purée it with the tahini and lemon juice.
3. Add the parsley and seasoning to the aubergine mixture.
4. Cut the tops off the tomatoes, remove the centre pulp and fill each tomato shell with the aubergine purée.
5. Place the tops back on the tomatoes and bake for 20 minutes at Gas Mark 5, 190°C or 375°F.

### Ingredients for Lentils and Spinach

*8 oz (225g) continental lentils*
*2 onions, chopped*
*1 lb (455g) fresh spinach or 8 oz (225g)*
 *frozen spinach, chopped*
*1 tablespoon lemon juice*
*1 teaspoon cumin powder*
*Seasoning*

### Method for Lentils and Spinach

1. Put the lentils and onions into a large pan with enough water to cover them and simmer for about 15 minutes.
2. Add the spinach and simmer for a further 20 minutes, adding the lemon juice, cumin and seasoning just before serving.

## Bean-and-rice-stuffed Marrow with Sesame Parsnips

*Ingredients for Bean-and-rice-stuffed Marrow*

1 marrow (about 2 lb [900g])
1 tablespoon vegetable oil
1 garlic clove (optional)
1 onion, finely chopped
1 teaspoon allspice powder
8 oz (225g) cooked beans, mashed coarsely
8 oz (225g) cooked long grain brown rice
2 oz (55g) walnuts, ground
1 oz (30g) dried prunes, soaked and cooked
1 tablespoon lemon juice
Seasoning

*Method for Bean-and-rice-stuffed Marrow*

1. Sauté the onion and garlic in the oil until the onion is tender.
2. Mix with the remaining filling ingredients.
3. Cut the marrow in half lengthways, remove and discard the pith so the skins form boats and fill each half with the bean and rice mixture.
4. Place the marrow halves in a dish, cover and bake at Gas Mark 6, 200°C or 400°F for about 30 minutes, or until the shell is tender.

*Ingredients for Sesame Parsnips*

1½ lb (680g) parsnips, cooked and mashed (still hot)
Spring onion, chopped
1 oz (30g) tahini
Fresh parsley, chopped
Seasoning
Sesame seeds

*Method for Sesame Parsnips*

1. Mix together the mashed parsnips, the spring onion, tahini, parsley and seasoning in a casserole dish.
2. Sprinkle the sesame seeds over the mixture and grill to crisp the top.

## Spiced-potato-stuffed Marrow with Cheese-topped Cabbage Masala

*Ingredients for Spiced-potato-stuffed Marr*

1 marrow (about 2 lb [900g])
2 tablespoons vegetable oil
1 large onion, finely chopped
1 lb (455g) potatoes, diced
1 teaspoon root ginger, grated
½ teaspoon chilli powder
½ teaspoon turmeric powder
4 oz (115g) frozen or fresh peas
4 tomatoes, chopped
Seasoning
Lemon juice

*Method for Spiced-potato-stuffed Marrow*

1. Remove a thin slice from each end of marrow, scoop out the centre pith and can remove the skin in alternative strip this looks attractive.
2. Fry the onion in the oil for a few minu add the potato and stir-fry for a few m minutes.
3. Add the spices, mix well and add the pe tomatoes and seasoning.
4. Simmer for about 10 minutes, or until potatoes are tender.
5. Add a squeeze of lemon juice to the fill mixture and stuff the centre of the marr
6. Cover with foil and bake at Gas Mark 180°C or 350°F for about 40 minu removing the foil occasionally to brush marrow with the juices.

*edients for Cheese-topped Cabbage Masala*

*(30ml) vegetable oil*
*(455g) firm cabbage, shredded*
*ions, chopped*
*spoons garam masala*
*oning*
*(85g) medium fat cheese, grated*

*od for Cheese-topped Cabbage Masala*

tir the cabbage and onion in the hot oil until
oated, add the garam masala, cover and
ently simmer, stirring occasionally.
eason to taste, pile into a dish, top with the
heese and grill to brown.

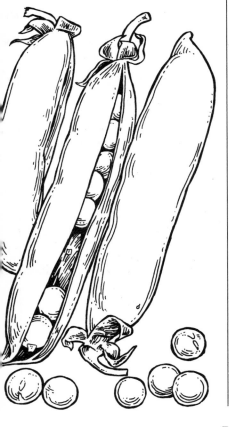

# Cheese and Courgette Charlotte with Orange, Raisin and Watercress Salad

### Ingredients for Cheese and Courgette Charlotte

*1 thick slice wholemeal bread, cubed*
*7 fl oz (200ml) skimmed milk*
*8 slices wholemeal bread, crusts removed*
*3 eggs, separated (beat the yolks and beat*
*    the whites until stiff)*
*4 oz (115g) cottage cheese*
*4 oz (115g) medium fat cheese, grated*
*1 large courgette, grated*
*1 tablespoon fresh or 1 teaspoon dried basil*
*Seasoning*
*1 small carton natural yogurt*

### Method for Cheese and Courgette Charlotte

1. Pour half of the milk over the bread cubes and sprinkle the remainder over the bread slices, leaving both to soak for 10 minutes.
2. Mix the beaten egg yolks with the soaked bread cubes and add the cheese, courgettes, basil and seasoning.
3. Add the yogurt to the mixture, blend well then fold in the stiffly beaten egg whites.
4. Line a dish with the soaked bread slices and pour in the cheese and vegetable filling, baking at Gas Mark 4, 180°C or 350°F for 35-40 minutes.

### Ingredients for Orange, Raisin and Watercress Salad

*Watercress*
*Carrot, grated*
*Spring onion, chopped*
*1 orange, peeled and chopped*
*1½ oz (45g) raisins*

### Method for Orange, Raisin and Watercress Salad

1. Mix all the ingredients together and serve.

## Sunflower and Sesame Loaf with New Potatoes in Spinach Sauce

*Ingredients for Sunflower and Sesame Loaf*

1 teaspoon yeast extract or soy sauce
4 oz (115g) fresh wholemeal breadcrumbs
4 oz (115g) sunflower seeds, ground
2 oz (55g) sesame seeds, lightly toasted
1 carrot, grated
1 stick of celery, finely chopped
1 onion, finely chopped
1 tablespoon fresh chopped or 1 teaspoon
   dried herbs
Seasoning

*Method for Sunflower and Sesame Loaf*

1. Mix the yeast extract or soy sauce with 4 fl
   oz (115ml) hot water and stir into the
   breadcrumbs.
2. Add the remaining ingredients and bake in
   a 1 lb (455g) loaf tin at Gas Mark 5, 190°C
   or 375°F for 40 minutes.

*Ingredients for New Potatoes in Spinach Sauce*

1 lb (455g) fresh or 8 oz (225g) frozen
   spinach, cooked
½ teaspoon nutmeg powder
1 small carton natural yogurt
Seasoning
1 lb (455g) new potatoes, cooked and still
   hot

*Method for New Potatoes in Spinach Sauce*

1. Liquidize the spinach, nutmeg, yogurt and
   seasoning, gently warm through and pour
   over the hot potatoes.

## Corn and Tomato Ba[ke] with Spicy Peas

*Ingredients for Corn and Tomato Bake*

2 medium onions, finely chopped
6 oz (170g) sweet corn, cooked or tinned
8 oz (225g) tomatoes, skinned and chopp[ed]
2 oz (55g) nuts, ground
6 oz (170g) fresh wholemeal breadcrumb[s]
2 tablespoons fresh parsley, chopped
1 teaspoon dried thyme
Rind of 1 lemon
2 eggs, beaten

*Method for Corn and Tomato Bake*

1. Mix all the ingredients together, adding
   beaten eggs last.
2. Pack into a dish and bake at Gas Mar[k]
   190°C or 375°F for 40 minutes.

*Ingredients for Spicy Peas*

½ oz (15ml) vegetable oil
1 onion, finely chopped
1 green chilli, sliced in half lengthways
2 lb (900g) fresh or frozen peas
Seasoning
1 tablespoon lemon juice
Lemon wedges

*Method for Spicy Peas*

1. Heat the oil in a pan and fry the onion u[ntil]
   tender, adding the chilli and frying [for]
   another minute.
2. Add the peas. Season and stir-fry for [a few]
   minutes over a gentle heat.
3. Serve with the lemon wedges and sprink[le]
   with the lemon juice.

# ut Pastry
# Mushroom Flan

*Ingredients*

*oz (170g) self-raising wholemeal flour*
*oz (30g) almonds, ground*
*oz (55g) vegetable margarine*
*3 fl oz (60-90ml) cold water*
*lb (455g) button mushrooms, chopped*
*tablespoon soy sauce or tomato purée*
*spring onions, chopped*
*teaspoon dried rosemary*
*asoning*
*oz (225g) quark or other low fat cheese*
*eggs, beaten*
*oz (30g) medium fat cheese, grated*

*ethod*

Mix the flour with the almonds and rub in the margarine to form crumbs.

Add sufficient water to form a soft dough and leave in the fridge for at least 30 minutes. Meanwhile, sauté the mushrooms in the soy sauce or tomato purée until tender and then add the onions, rosemary and seasoning.

Beat the eggs into the quark or low fat cheese and add to the mushrooms.

Roll out the pastry between polythene sheets, remove the polythene and line a flan tin. Pour the mushroom mixture into the flan case and top with the cheese.

Bake at Gas Mark 5, 190°C or 375°F for 40 minutes.

# Spinach and
# Cheese Pie

*Ingredients*

*6 oz (170g) wholemeal flour*
*2 oz (55g) chick-pea flour*
*¾ teaspoon baking powder*
*Pinch salt*
*3 oz (85g) vegetable margarine*
*4 fl oz (115ml) cold water*
*1 lb (455g) fresh or 8 oz (225g) frozen*
  *spinach, lightly cooked*
*4 oz (115g) cottage cheese*
*4 spring onions, chopped*
*¼ teaspoon nutmeg*
*Seasoning*
*1 egg, beaten*

*Method*

1. Sift the flours, baking powder, salt and add back the bran.
2. Rub the margarine into the flour to form crumbs, adding sufficient water to make a soft dough. Leave in the fridge for about 30 minutes.
3. Chop the spinach and mix with the remaining ingredients.
4. Divide the pastry in two and roll out between polythene sheets to make two 8 inch (20cm) squares. Remove polythene.
5. Place one pastry square in an 8 inch (20cm) tin, cover with the filling and lightly press down the other pastry layer on top.
6. Prick the top of the pie and bake at Gas Mark 5, 190°C or 375°F for 35 minutes. (As an alternative you could try substituting 1 lb (455g) grated courgettes for the spinach and chopped fresh mint for the nutmeg.)

## Yogurt Scone Ratatouille Pizza with Bean and Nut Salad

*Ingredients for Yogurt Scone Ratatouille Pizza*

8 oz (225g) wholemeal flour
1 teaspoon bicarbonate of soda
1 teaspoon mustard powder
Seasoning
1 oz (30g) vegetable margarine
1 small carton natural yogurt
1 15 oz (425g) tin ratatouille
1 oz (30g) Parmesan cheese

*Method for Yogurt Scone Ratatouille Pizza*

1. Sift together the flour, bicarbonate of soda, mustard, seasoning and then add back the bran.
2. Rub the margarine into the flour mixture to form crumbs and add the yogurt, mixing to make a soft dough.
3. Roll or press out the dough to ½ inch (1.25cm) thickness and bake in a shallow tin for 10 minutes at Gas Mark 7, 220°C or 425°F.
4. Spread the ratatouille over the base, sprinkle the Parmesan over and return to the oven for 10 minutes to melt the topping.

*Ingredients for Bean and Nut Salad*

'Free' vegetables of your choice
4 oz (115g) cooked beans or 1 15 oz (425g) tinned beans
1 oz (30g) nuts, toasted and chopped

*Method for Bean and Nut Salad*

1. Mix all the ingredients together and serve.

## Macaroni Cheese and Vegetable Casserole with Ginger and Garlic Carrots (serves 6)

*Ingredients for Macaroni Cheese and Vegetable Casserole*

1 lb (455g) wholemeal macaroni
1 oz (30g) wholemeal flour
15 fl oz (425ml) skimmed milk
4 oz (115g) medium fat cheese, grated
4 oz (115g) button mushrooms, sliced
1 green pepper, deseeded and chopped
4 oz (115g) fresh or frozen peas
½ teaspoon mace powder
2 eggs, beaten
Seasoning

*Method for Macaroni Cheese and Vegetable Casserole*

1. Cook the macaroni in boiling water until just tender.
2. Make a paste with the flour and a little of the cold milk.
3. Heat the rest of the milk, then slowly add to the paste, stirring continuously. Return milk and flour mixture to the heat, still stirring, to thicken.
4. Stir the cheese into the sauce, followed by the vegetables, spices, seasoning and finally the beaten eggs.
5. Transfer to a casserole dish and bake at Gas Mark 5, 190°C or 375°F for 30 minutes.

*Ingredients for Ginger and Garlic Carrots*

1 tablespoon cumin seeds
1½ lb (680g) carrots, sliced
1 garlic clove, crushed
1 inch (2.5cm) root ginger, grated
2 tablespoons lemon juice

thod for Ginger and Garlic Carrots

Lightly toast the cumin seeds.
Cook the carrots until just tender. Drain.
Stir the lemon juice, mixed with the garlic
and ginger, into the carrots and sprinkle
cumin seeds over them and serve.

## egetable and Millet
## e with Cucumber
## nd Herbs

*redients for Vegetable and Millet Pie*

*z (225g) each carrots, turnips (or swedes)
and parsnips, diced into similarly sized
pieces
mall fennel, sliced
oint (285ml) dry cider
ablespoon fresh or 1 teaspoon dried
thyme
soning
z (225g) millet
nion, finely chopped
pints (850ml) vegetable stock or water
z (115g) tofu or cottage cheese, mashed
z (55g) hazelnuts, toasted and ground
mall carton natural yogurt*

*thod for Vegetable and Millet Pie*

Place the vegetables, cider, thyme and
seasoning in a saucepan and cook, covered,
for about 20 minutes, or until the vegetables
are just tender.
Meanwhile, cook the millet and onion in the
vegetable stock in a covered pan for 20
minutes. Remove from the heat and leave to
stand for about 10 minutes to allow all of the
liquid to be absorbed.
Stir the tofu and nuts into the millet.
Stir the yogurt into the slightly cooled
vegetables and pile into a large dish.
Top the vegetables with the millet mixture

and bake at Gas Mark 5, 190°C or 375°F
for about 25 minutes.

*Ingredients for Cucumber and Herbs*

*1 cucumber, diced
1 onion, thinly sliced
½ oz (15g) vegetable oil
2 tablespoons fresh herbs (e.g. rosemary,
    marjoram) chopped
½ teaspoon Tabasco sauce
Seasoning*

*Method for Cucumber and Herbs*

1. Heat the oil in a pan, and stir-fry the
   cucumber and onion for a few minutes.
2. Sprinkle in the herbs, Tabasco sauce and
   seasoning, cover and simmer over a low heat
   for 5 minutes, shaking the pan occasionally.

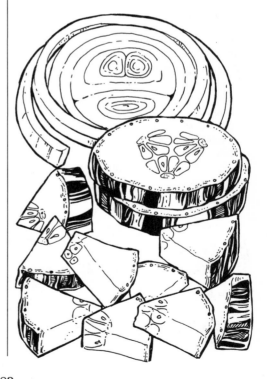

# Cauliflower, Leek and Hazelnut Casserole with Red Kidney Bean and Courgette Salad

### Ingredients for Cauliflower, Leek and Hazelnut Casserole

1 cauliflower, broken into small florets
2 leeks, sliced
5 fl oz (140ml) skimmed milk or soy milk
4 oz (115g) quark or tofu
Pinch dried dill weed
Seasoning
4 oz (115g) hazelnuts, ground or chopped
2 oz (55g) fresh wholemeal breadcrumbs
1 oz (30g) vegetable margarine, melted

### Method for Cauliflower, Leek and Hazelnut Casserole

1. Steam the cauliflower and leeks together until just tender then drain off any liquid.
2. Blend the milk, quark or tofu, dill weed and seasoning and add half of the hazelnuts.
3. Pour the quark or tofu mixture over the vegetables in a casserole dish and top with the rest of the hazelnuts, mixed with the breadcrumbs and melted margarine.
4. Bake at Gas Mark 4, 180°C or 350°F for about 15 minutes, or until the top is crispy and brown.

### Ingredients for Red Kidney Bean and Courgette Salad

4 oz (115g) cooked red kidney beans or 1 15 oz (425g) tin, drained
1 lb (455g) courgettes, sliced and lightly cooked
2 oz (55g) spring onions, chopped
Fresh herbs, chopped
Seasoning
2 tablespoons mayonnaise
Juice of 1 lemon
Watercress

### Method for Red Kidney Bean and Courgette Salad

1. Mix together all of the ingredients, except the watercress, which can be used as a bo▶ for the salad.

0 Calories Approximately
r Portion

## anut, Sesame and
## pple Burgers with
## urried Salad

*redients for Peanut, Sesame and
ole Burgers*

z (225g) fresh wholemeal breadcrumbs
z (115g) tahini
z (115g) peanuts, ground
nions, grated
pples, grated
easpoon coriander powder
easpoons lemon juice
asoning

*thod for Peanut, Sesame and
ole Burgers*

Mix all the ingredients together well.
Form into firm burgers and fry on both sides.

*redients for Curried Salad*

ee' vegetables of your choice
iblespoons mayonnaise
non juice
teaspoons curry powder
asoning

*thod for Curried Salad*

Chop and mix together the 'free' vegetables.
Mix together well the mayonnaise, lemon
juice, curry powder and seasoning.
Pour the curried dressing over the vegetables.

## Coconut and Rice Squares with Mixed Bean Salad

*Ingredients for Coconut and Rice Squares*

2 oz (55g) creamed coconut
1 pint (570ml) vegetable stock or water
12 oz (340g) long grain brown rice
1 teaspoon dried mixed herbs
1 teaspoon garam masala
1 courgette, finely grated
1 small red pepper, finely chopped
Spring onions, finely chopped
Seasoning

*Method for Coconut and Rice Squares*

1. Bring the stock to the boil, add the creamed
   coconut to dissolve it, followed by the rice,
   herbs and garam masala.
2. Cook the rice gently, covered, for 35 minutes
   or until tender.
3. Add the vegetables a few minutes before the
   end of the cooking time, and season.
4. Transfer the rice mixture to a square dish,
   cover with a plate, weight down and let cool.
5. Cut into squares and serve cold.

*Ingredients for Mixed Bean Salad*

Tomatoes
Spring onion
Parsley
Lemon juice
Seasoning
12 oz (340g) cooked or tinned mixed beans
Nutmeg

*Method for Mixed Bean Salad*

1. Mix together the tomatoes, spring onion,
   parsley, lemon juice and seasoning.
2. Add the beans and sprinkle with nutmeg to
   serve.

# Dolly's Burgers with Tomatoes and Potatoes in Cheese Sauce

## Ingredients for Dolly's Burgers

1 lb (455g) carrots, grated
2 onions, finely chopped
4 sticks of celery, finely chopped
4 tablespoons cabbage or Brussels sprouts
   or fresh spinach, finely chopped
2 oz (55g) fresh wholemeal breadcrumbs
5 oz (140g) hazelnuts, ground
2 tablespoons fresh herbs (mint, lovage,
   marjoram, thyme or parsley), chopped
½ teaspoon nutmeg or mace powder
2 tablespoons tomato purée
1 egg, beaten
Seasoning

## Method for Dolly's Burgers

1. Mix all the ingredients together very well and squeeze and shape to form firm burgers.
2. Bake at Gas Mark 5, 190°C or 375°F for 45 minutes.

## Ingredients for Tomatoes and Potatoes in Cheese Sauce

1 lb (455g) potatoes
1 pint (570ml) skimmed milk
2 oz (55g) wholemeal flour
2 oz (55g) medium fat cheese, grated
Spring onions, chopped
Seasoning
1 lb (455g) tomatoes, quartered
Fresh parsley, chopped, to garnish

## Method for Tomatoes and Potatoes in Cheese Sauce

1. Cut the potatoes into even size pieces and cook.
2. Make a paste with the flour and a little of the milk, heat the rest of the milk and gradually add it to the paste, stirring continuousl[y]
3. Return the milk and flour mixture to the he[at] and stir until thickened.
4. Add the cheese, onions and seasoning to t[he] sauce, followed by the tomatoes and cook[ed] potatoes.
5. Heat through only and then serve, garnish[ed] with the chopped parsley. (Alternatively, se[rve] the tomatoes separately, grilled.)

# Rice-stuffed Cabbage Leaves Baked in Coconut Sauce with Fried Tofu

## Ingredients

1 large cabbage
1 oz (30g) vegetable margarine
2 onions, chopped
1 garlic clove, crushed
6 oz (170g) button mushrooms, chopped
8 oz (225g) cooked long grain brown rice
3 oz (85g) hazelnuts, ground
1 oz (30g) pine nuts
½ teaspoon ground ginger
Seasoning
10 fl oz (285ml) vegetable stock, boiling
4 oz (115g) dessicated coconut
8 oz (225g) firm tofu

## Method

1. Boil the cabbage whole for about 10 minut[es] or until tender.
2. Drain, remove the outer larger leaves and s[et] them aside.
3. Fry the onion and garlic in the margari[ne] for 5 minutes, add the mushrooms, cooki[ng] for a few more minutes and stirri[ng] occasionally.
4. Add the rice, nuts, pine nuts, ginger a[nd]

— 86 —

seasoning to the mushrooms.

Spread out the cabbage leaves and spoon 2-3 tablespoons of the filling on one end of the leaf, fold in the sides and roll up to form an envelope.

Repeat with the other leaves until all of the filling is used up and arrange the stuffed leaves in a large, shallow dish.

Make the coconut sauce by beating the boiling water into the coconut until the mixture is smooth and thick.

Pour the coconut sauce around the cabbage leaves, cover and bake at Gas Mark 2, 160°F or 300°F for 1 hour.

Serve with fried firm tofu chunks.

# Cracked-wheat-stuffed peppers with Mixed Vegetable Salad and Peanut Sauce

### Ingredients for Cracked-wheat-stuffed Peppers

*peppers*
*onion*
*pint (285ml) tomato juice*
*oz (85g) cracked wheat*
*oz (85g) nuts, ground*
*teaspoon cinnamon*
*asoning*
*esh parsley, chopped*

### Method for Cracked-wheat-stuffed Peppers

Boil the peppers for a few minutes.

Cut off and keep the tops, but discard the centre pith and seeds.

Meanwhile, simmer the cracked wheat, onion and tomato juice for 20 minutes, add the remaining ingredients and fill each pepper.

Replace the pepper tops, place in a dish, cover and bake at Gas Mark 6, 200°C or 400°F for 30 minutes.

### Ingredients for Mixed Vegetable Salad

*'Free' vegetables of your choice*
*Lemon juice*
*Herbs*
*Seasoning*
*10 oz (285g) cooked potatoes, diced*
*8 oz (225g) cooked or tinned chick-peas*

### Method for Mixed Vegetable Salad

1. Chop the 'free' vegetables.
2. Mix them together with the other ingredients and serve with or without the Peanut Sauce as you prefer.

### Ingredients for Peanut Sauce

*½ oz (15g) creamed coconut*
*½ pint (285ml) boiling water or vegetable stock*
*4 oz (115g) peanuts, roasted*
*Seasoning*

### Method for Peanut Sauce

1. Dissolve the coconut in the boiling water.
2. Liquidize all the ingredients together to form a paste, and simmer for a few minutes.
3. Serve the sauce hot with the stuffed peppers or cold with the Mixed Vegetable Salad.

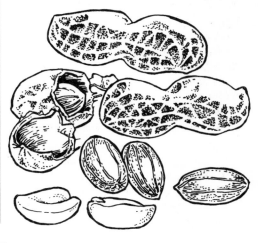

## Chick-pea-stuffed Aubergines with Cauliflower in Tahini Sauce

### Ingredients for Chick-pea-stuffed Aubergines

2 large aubergines
2 onions, finely chopped
1 oz (30g) vegetable oil
12 oz (340g) cooked chick-peas, mashed
4 oz (115g) cooked long grain brown rice
1 lb (455g) fresh tomatoes, skinned and chopped
2 tablespoons fresh mint chopped or 2 teaspoons dried mint
Seasoning

### Method for Chick-pea-stuffed Aubergines

1. Boil the aubergine for 2 minutes.
2. Cut in half lengthways, carefully remove the flesh and chop.
3. Sauté the onion and aubergine flesh in the oil, until both are tender.
4. Mix with the remaining ingredients, pile into the aubergine halves and bake covered for 45 minutes at Gas Mark 4, 180°C or 350°F.

### Ingredients for Cauliflower in Tahini Sauce

1 large cauliflower, broken into small florets
1 large onion, chopped
2 tablespoons soy sauce
10 oz (285g) silken tofu
4 oz (115g) tahini
Seasoning
Fresh parsley to garnish

### Method for Cauliflower in Tahini Sauce

1. Simmer the cauliflower and onion in the soy sauce in a covered pan until tender.
2. Blend the tofu, tahini and seasoning in a liquidizer. Gently warm the sauce before pouring over the cauliflower and garnishing with parsley.

## Courgette, Tofu and Nut Bake with Creamy Brussels Sprouts

### Ingredients for Courgette, Tofu and Nut Bake

2 onions, finely chopped
1 lb (455g) courgettes, grated
1 large carrot, grated
½ oz (15g) tomato purée
2 teaspoons dried mixed herbs
6 oz (170g) fresh wholemeal breadcrumbs
10 oz (285g) packet tofu, drained and mashed
4 oz (115g) nuts, ground
2 oz (55g) dessicated coconut
Seasoning

### Method for Courgette, Tofu and Nut Bake

1. Simmer onions, courgettes, carrot and tomato purée in a covered pan until the onion is tender.
2. Mix the vegetables with all the other ingredients, pack into a large cake tin casserole dish and bake at Gas Mark 5, 190°C or 375°F for 40 minutes.
3. Cool a little if turning the bake out.

### Ingredients for Creamy Brussels Sprouts

1½ lbs (680g) Brussels sprouts
2 small cartons natural yogurt
Fresh chives, chopped
Fresh parsley, chopped
Seasoning

### Method for Creamy Brussels Sprouts

1. Cook the Brussels sprouts until just tender and then drain.
2. Gently heat the yogurt, herbs and seasoning and pour over the Brussels sprouts.

# Mary's Chick-pea Savoury with Mushroom Sauce

### Ingredients for Mary's Chick-pea Savoury

*8 oz (225g) chick-peas, soaked and cooked*
*8 oz (225g) hazelnuts, ground*
*1 onion, chopped*
*1 carrot, grated*
*2 sticks of celery, finely chopped*
*1 tomato, chopped*
*1 dessertspoon dried marjoram*
*1 dessertspoon dried oregano*
*1 egg, beaten*
*1 small carton natural yogurt*
*2 tablespoons soy sauce*
*seasoning*
*parsley or chopped tomato to garnish*

### Method for Mary's Chick-pea Savoury

1. Purée the chick-peas in a blender and mix well with the nuts, vegetables and herbs.
2. Mix together the egg, yogurt, soy sauce and 4 fl oz (115ml) water, stir into the chick-pea mixture and season well.
3. Pile into a dish or tin, cover with greaseproof paper and bake at Gas Mark 6, 200°C or 400°F for 45 minutes, removing the paper before the end of the cooking time to brown the top.
4. Garnish with parsley or tomato.

### Ingredients for Mushroom Sauce

*1 lb (455g) mushrooms, lightly cooked*
*1 bay leaf*
*1 oz (30g) wholemeal flour*
*1 teaspoon yeast extract*

### Method for Mushroom Sauce

1. Purée the mushrooms, make up to nearly 1 pint (570ml) with vegetable stock or water, add the bay leaf and bring nearly to the boil.
2. Mix the flour with a little cold water to form a paste and gradually stir in the hot purée.
3. Return to the heat, add the yeast extract and continue to stir while the mixture thickens.
4. Serve the Chick-pea Savoury and Mushroom Sauce with a green 'free' vegetable, such as broccoli or runner beans, lightly cooked.

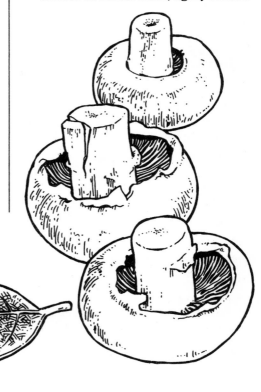

# Curried Mushroom Ring with Potato and Cheese Layer

*Ingredients for Curried Mushroom Ring*

12 oz (340g) mushrooms, chopped
1 tablespoon soy sauce
1 onion, finely chopped
5 oz (140g) nuts, ground
5 oz (140g) fresh wholemeal breadcrumbs
1 apple, grated
1 tablespoon curry powder
1 teaspoon dried mixed herbs
Seasoning

*Method for Curried Mushroom Ring*

1. Sauté the mushrooms and onions in the soy sauce to cook a little.
2. Mix with all the other ingredients and add a little water if the mixture seems too dry.
3. Pack into a ring mould, cover with foil and bake at Gas Mark 5, 190°C or 375°F for 30 minutes, removing the foil towards the end of the cooking time to brown the top.
4. Fill with some 'free' vegetables to serve, e.g. chopped tomatoes.

*Ingredients for Potato and Cheese Layer*

½ oz (15g) vegetable margarine
1 lb (455g) potatoes, thinly sliced
3 oz (85g) medium fat cheese, grated
8 oz (225g) onions, thinly sliced
Seasoning

*Method for Potato and Cheese Layer*

1. Melt the margarine in a large frying pan and remove from the heat.
2. Arrange half the potatoes, overlapping, in the bottom of the pan, season, sprinkle the cheese over the potato layer, following this with the onion and season again.
3. Add the final layer of potatoes, cover and cook over a moderate heat for 20 minutes
4. Invert the mixture on to a plate, slip it back into the pan and cook the other side for about 20 minutes or until all of the 'cake' i tender.

# Pasties with Cauliflower and Peanut Salad

*Ingredients for Pasties*

8 oz (225g) wholemeal flour
½ teaspoon baking powder
1 teaspoon cumin powder
Pinch salt
3 oz (85g) vegetable margarine
1 oz (30g) low fat spread
3-4 fl oz (90-115ml) cold water
8 oz (225g) cooked potato, mashed
4 oz (115g) fresh or frozen peas
4 oz (115g) carrot, grated
1 onion, grated or chopped
Juice of ½ lemon
1 teaspoon coriander powder
½ teaspoon each ginger and mustard powder
Seasoning

*Method for Pasties*

1. Make the pastry by sifting the dry ingredient together and adding back the bran.
2. Mix in the fat to make crumbs and ad sufficient water to form a moist dough. Leave in the fridge for at least 30 minutes.
3. Mix all of the filling ingredients together well
4. Roll out the pastry between sheets of polythene, remove the polythene and cut into four 6-7 inch (15-18cm) diameter rounds.
5. Place a quarter of the filling in each round Season well, dampen the edges with wate

and draw the sides up to the top.

5. Crimp the pasty join, prick lightly with a fork and bake at Gas Mark 7, 220°C or 425°F for 25 minutes.

### Ingredients for Cauliflower and Peanut Salad

*1 cauliflower, cooked and broken into small florets*
*1½ oz (45g) salted peanuts*
*Spring onions, chopped*
*Watercress*
*Lemon juice*
*Pinch dried dill weed*
*Seasoning*

### Method for Cauliflower and Peanut Salad

1. Mix all the ingredients together and serve.

# Sweet Corn Pizza with Minted Courgette and Yogurt Salad

### Ingredients for Sweet Corn Pizza

*6 oz (170g) self-raising wholemeal flour*
*3 oz (85g) vegetable margarine*
*4 oz (115g) cooked potato, mashed*
*6 oz (170g) sweet corn, tinned or cooked*
*1 green pepper, deseeded and chopped*
*8 oz (225g) tomatoes, chopped*
*Spring onions, chopped*
*½ teaspoon dried basil*
*Seasoning*
*6 oz (170g) curd cheese*

### Method for Sweet Corn Pizza

1. Sift the flour, add back the bran and mix in the margarine to form crumbs.
2. Knead in the potato and add a little cold water to form a stiff dough.

3. Roll out the dough between polythene sheets to fit an 8 inch (20cm) tin.
4. Mix the remaining ingredients together, reserving half the tomatoes.
5. Spread the mixture over the pizza base, top with the reserved tomatoes and bake at Gas Mark 7, 220°C or 425°F for 35 minutes.

### Ingredients for Minted Courgette and Yogurt Salad

*1 lb (455g) courgettes, grated*
*2 small cartons natural yogurt*
*1 tablespoon mayonnaise*
*1 tablespoon fresh mint chopped or 1 teaspoon dried mint*
*Seasoning*
*Lettuce or watercress*

### Method for Minted Courgette and Yogurt Salad

1. Mix together the courgettes, mayonnaise, mint and seasoning.
2. Pile on to a bed of lettuce or watercress.

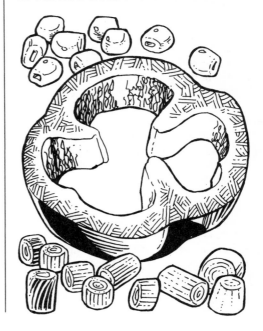

## Mexican Bean-topped Corn Pizza

### Ingredients

6 oz (170g) wholemeal flour
3 oz (85g) fine maize flour
2 teaspoons baking powder
Pinch salt
4 oz (115g) low fat spread
4 fl oz (115ml) skimmed milk
8 oz (225g) tomatoes, skinned and chopped
1 onion, finely chopped
½ green pepper, chopped
4 oz (115g) mushrooms, chopped
1 garlic clove, crushed
Pinch chilli powder
Seasoning
4 oz (115g) red kidney beans, cooked, or 1
    15 oz (425g) tin, drained
2 spring onions, chopped
1 oz (30g) black olives, stoned
4 oz (115g) medium fat cheese, grated

### Method

1. Sift the flours, baking powder and salt and add back the bran.
2. Rub in the margarine to form crumbs and add sufficient milk to make a soft dough. Leave in the fridge while following step 3.
3. Meanwhile, simmer the tomatoes, onion, pepper, mushrooms, garlic, chilli powder and seasoning for about 20-25 minutes, until the onion is tender and the liquid has reduced.
4. Roll out the dough to cover a 13-14 inch (33-35cm) pizza tin and pinch the edges to form a rim.
5. Add the kidney beans to the tomatoes and spread the mixture over the pizza base.
6. Top the pizza with the spring onions and olives, followed by the grated cheese.
7. Bake at Gas Mark 6, 200°C or 400°F for 20 minutes.

## Mushroom and Cashew Nut Rice

### Ingredients

12 oz (340g) long grain brown rice
1 onion, chopped
1 garlic clove, crushed
15 fl oz (425ml) vegetable stock or water
8 fl oz (240ml) dry white wine
8 oz (225g) button mushrooms, chopped
1 lb (455g) fresh tomatoes, skinned and
    chopped, or 1 15 oz (425g) tin of
    tomatoes
1 tablespoon fresh oregano, chopped, or
    1 teaspoon dried oregano
Seasoning
4 oz (115g) cashew nuts, lightly toasted and
    chopped or halved
Fresh parsley, chopped, to garnish

### Method

1. Place the rice, onion, garlic, vegetable stock or water and wine in a saucepan bring to the boil, stir once and then simmer, covered, for 40 minutes or until the rice is cooked and the liquid has been absorbed.
2. Meanwhile, cook the mushrooms, tomatoes herbs and seasoning together for about 15 minutes.
3. Stir the nuts into the rice, arrange in a ring on a large plate and fill the centre with the tomato mixture, garnishing with parsley.

# Fruity Bean Stew with Wholemeal Rolls

*Ingredients*

*8 oz (225g) haricot beans, soaked and
    drained
4 pints (2.3l) vegetable stock or water
1 lb (455g) fresh or frozen French beans
1 lb (455g) carrots, diced
1 red pepper, deseeded and chopped
2 onions, sliced
8 fl oz (240ml) dry cider
½ teaspoon each grated nutmeg, dried
    marjoram and basil
1 lb (455g) cooking apples peeled, cored
    and diced
1 banana, sliced
2 oz (55g) pineapple, drained from natural
    juice
2 oz (55g) prunes, soaked and stoned
4 wholemeal rolls
2 oz (55g) peanut butter*

*Method*

1. Cook the beans in half the stock or water until tender.
2. Add the rest of the stock, the French beans, carrots, pepper and onion and simmer until the vegetables are tender.
3. Add the cider, spices and apple, bring to the boil then simmer for 10 minutes.
4. Add the banana, pineapple and prunes, simmering for a further 5 minutes.
5. Serve hot, accompanied by wholemeal rolls, spread with the peanut butter.

# Aubergine and Red Kidney Bean Casserole with Spinach Rice

*Ingredients for Aubergine and Red Kidney Bean Casserole*

*8 oz (225g) red kidney beans, cooked
1 onion, finely chopped
1 garlic clove
4 sticks of celery, chopped
1 large aubergine, diced
1 green pepper, deseeded and chopped
½ oz (15g) tomato purée
6 fl oz (170ml) unsweetened apple juice
6 fl oz (170ml) vegetable stock or water
1 teaspoon dried oregano
Seasoning
Mustard and cress to garnish*

*Method for Aubergine and Red Kidney Bean Casserole*

1. Mix all the ingredients together, except for the mustard and cress, pile into a casserole dish, cover and bake at Gas Mark 4, 180°C or 350°F for about 1½ hours.
2. Garnish with mustard and cress to serve.

*Ingredients for Spinach Rice*

*12 oz (340g) long grain brown rice, cooked
1 lb (455g) fresh spinach or 8 oz (225g)
    frozen spinach, lightly cooked and
    chopped
3 spring onions, chopped
Seasoning*

*Method for Spinach Rice*

1. Mix the hot rice with the spinach, onions and seasoning, heating through if necessary.

## Treats — Index

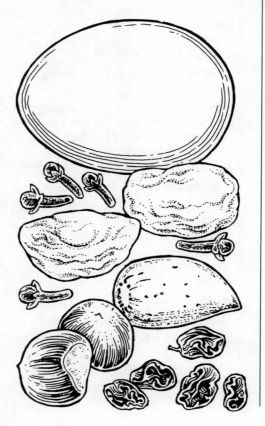

## Treats

# Nutty Shortbread

(1,700 cals approximately)

*Ingredients*

*1 oz (30g) raisins or sultanas*
*2 oz (55g) nuts, chopped*
*1 tablespoon unsweetened apple juice*
*5 oz (140g) wholemeal flour*
*1 oz (30g) rolled oats*
*1 oz (30g) fructose*
*2 oz (55g) vegetable margarine*
*2 oz (55g) low fat spread*

*Method*

1. Mix the fruit and nuts with the apple juice.
2. Combine the dry ingredients, then rub in the fat to form a crumbly mixture.
3. Stir in the fruit and nut mixture and knead to make a dough.
4. Press the mixture into an 8 inch (20cm) square tin and prick the surface. Bake at Gas Mark 4, 180°C or 350°F for 20 minutes, or until lightly browned at the edges.
5. Slice when cool.

# Carob Brownies

(1,700 cals approximately)

*Ingredients*

*4 oz (115g) low fat spread*
*1 oz (30g) carob powder*
*2 oz (55g) raisins or sultanas*
*8 oz (225g) wholemeal or muesli or oat or
    digestive biscuits (about 15), crushed*
*1 teaspoon mixed spice*

**Method**

1. Melt the fat, remove from the heat and stir in the carob powder.
2. Add the raisins, crushed biscuits and mixed spice, mixing well.
3. Press the mixture into a shallow tin or container, chill and slice.

# Iris' Cookies

(970 cals approximately)

*Ingredients*

*1 large egg, beaten*
*2 oz (55g) fructose*
*½ teaspoon baking powder*
*2 oz (55g) almonds, ground*
*4 oz (115g) wholemeal semolina*
*Grated rind of 1 lemon*
*A little orange flower water or water*

*Method*

1. Mix all the ingredients together well, except for the orange flower water.
2. Wet hands with the orange flower water (or simply water) and roll pieces of the mixture into large, marble-size balls.
3. Place the balls on a greased baking sheet, well apart, and bake at Gas Mark 4, 180°C or 350°F for 10-12 minutes until they start to become golden.
4. Cool on a rack.

# Fruit and Nut Balls

(1,400 cals approximately)

*Ingredients*

*8 oz (225g) dried fruit (dates, sultanas, raisins, currants)*
*3 oz (85g) nuts*
*1 oz (30g) honey*
*Lemon juice*
*1 teaspoon cinnamon*
*2 oz (55g) dessicated coconut*

*Method*

1. Mix the fruit and nuts in a blender.
2. Add the honey, lemon juice and cinnamon to the fruit and nuts and mix well.
3. Form into small balls, roll in the coconut and chill.

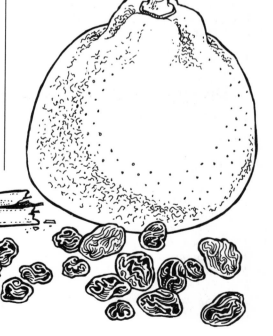

# Carob Cake
(2,040 cals approximately)

### Ingredients

5 oz (140g) low fat spread
4 oz (115g) fructose
3 eggs, beaten
8 oz (225g) self-raising wholemeal flour
1 oz (30g) carob powder
3 tablespoons skimmed milk
2 oz (55g) whole fruit jam of your choice

### Method

1. Cream the fat and fructose until light and fluffy.
2. Add the eggs, mix well, and then fold in the flour and carob.
3. Stir in sufficient milk to give a dropping consistency.
4. Divide the mixture between two 7 inch (18cm) sandwich tins and bake at Gas Mark 4, 180°C or 350°F for 25 minutes.
5. Cool on wire racks and, when cool, sandwich together with the jam.

# Date and Walnut Cake
(2,560 cals approximately)

### Ingredients

6 oz (170g) dates, chopped
6 fl oz (170ml) skimmed milk
2 oz (55g) vegetable margarine
2 fl oz (55ml) vegetable oil
2 eggs
6 oz (170g) wholemeal flour
1½ teaspoons baking powder
1 teaspoon mixed spice
1 teaspoon ginger powder
2 oz (55g) rolled oats
2 oz (55g) walnuts, chopped
Grated rind of 1 lemon

### Method

1. Bring the dates and milk to the boil and then leave to cool.
2. Blend half the date mixture, margarine, oil and eggs in a blender.
3. Mix together the flour, baking powder, mixed spice, ginger, oats, walnuts and lemon rind and then stir in the date and egg mixture.
4. Add the remaining dates, pack into a 2 lb (900g) loaf tin and bake at Gas Mark 3, 160°C or 325°F for about 1 hour or until when a knife is inserted it comes out clean.
5. Cool a little in the tin before turning out on to a rack.

# Carrot and Pineapple Cake (1,930 cals approximately)

### Ingredients

7 oz (200g) carrot, finely grated
2½ fl oz (75ml) vegetable oil
2 eggs, beaten
Almond essence
7 oz (200g) pineapple, drained well from natural juice and liquidized
5 oz (140g) wholemeal flour
2 oz (55g) almonds, ground
1½ oz (45g) dessicated coconut
1 teaspoon baking powder
2 teaspoons cinnamon

### Method

1. Mix the carrots, oil and beaten eggs together.
2. Stir in a few drops of almond essence and the liquidized pineapple.
3. Sift the dry ingredients together, add back the bran and stir into the carrot and pineapple mixture.
4. Bake at Gas Mark 3, 160°C or 325°F for 1¼ hours, or until when a knife is inserted it comes out clean. Cool on a rack.

# Hazelnut Teabread
(1,960 cals approximately)

### Ingredients

1 egg, beaten
3 fl oz (90ml) vegetable oil
Grated rind of 1 lemon
1 small carton natural yogurt
6 oz (170g) self-raising wholemeal flour
1 oz (30g) All Bran
1 teaspoon allspice
Pinch salt
1 teaspoon bicarbonate of soda
4 oz (115g) hazelnuts, coarsely ground

### Method

1. Beat together the egg, oil, lemon rind and yogurt.
2. Combine the remaining ingredients and stir into the yogurt mixture until well blended.
3. Spoon into a 1 lb (455g) loaf tin and bake at Gas Mark 5, 190°C or 375°F for about 1 hour, leaving it to cool before turning out.

# Apple and Yogurt Scone Round
(1,100 cals approximately)

### Ingredients

2 oz (55g) low fat spread
8 oz (225g) wholemeal self-raising flour
1 teaspoon baking powder
Pinch salt
1 teaspoon cinnamon
1 large eating apple, grated
1 small carton natural yogurt

### Method

1. Rub the fat into the flour, salt, baking powder and cinnamon, then add the apple.
2. Mix in the yogurt to form a soft dough and roll or press out to ½ inch (1cm) thickness.
3. Shape into a round, score to divide and bake on a tray at Gas Mark 6, 200°C or 400°F for 25 minutes, cooling on a wire rack.

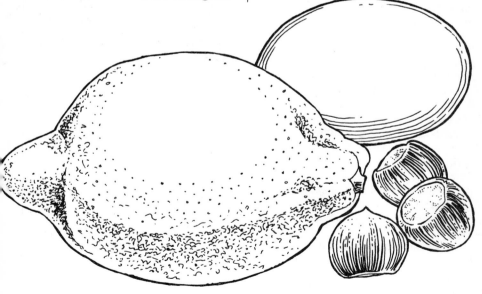

## Apricot and Almond Squares
(1,950 cals approximately)

### Ingredients

4 oz (115g) wholemeal flour
½ teaspoon baking powder
2 oz (55g) low fat spread
8 oz (225g) dried apricots, soaked overnight
    in 1 pint (570ml) cold tea
3 oz (85g) almonds, ground
3 oz (85g) dessicated coconut
1 egg, beaten
Almond essence

### Method

1. Make the pastry by first sifting the flour and baking powder, adding back the bran.
2. Then rub in the margarine to form crumbs, add sufficient cold water to make a soft dough and leave in the fridge while the apricots are cooking.
3. Simmer apricots in the soaking liquid until soft — about 30 minutes — and coarsely mash them.
4. Roll out the pastry between sheets of polythene, remove the polythene, then line an 8-9 inch (19-23cm) square tin, prick well and bake blind for 10 minutes at Gas Mark 6, 200°C or 400°F.
5. Mix together the almonds and coconut, stir in the beaten egg, a few drops of almond essence and 3 oz (85g) of the mashed apricots.
6. Spread the remaining apricots over the pastry case, cover with the almond, coconut and apricot mixture and bake at Gas Mark 5, 190°C or 375°F for 15 minutes to set the top.
7. Leave to cool before cutting into slices.

## Fruit Cheesecake
(950 cals approximately)

### Ingredients

3 oz (85g) wholemeal biscuits, crushed
8 oz (225g) quark or tofu
2 soft pears or 1 large banana
1 teaspoon lemon juice
4 fl oz (115ml) skimmed milk
2 eggs, separated
Grated rind of 1 lemon
1 oz (30g) raisins or sultanas

### Method

1. Spread the biscuits over the bottom of a loose-bottomed shallow cake tin.
2. Blend the quark or tofu, fruit, lemon juice, milk and egg yolks in a liquidizer. Stir in the lemon rind, raisins and stiffly beaten egg whites.
3. Bake at Gas Mark 4, 170°C or 350°F for 20 minutes or until the cake is set.

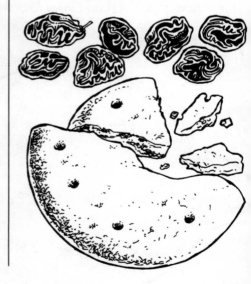

# ⌄weet Couscous Cake

(200 cals approximately)

*⌐redients*

*⌐z (170g) couscous*
*⌐pint (200ml) hot water*
*⌐z (55g) dried fruit*
*⌐ce of 1 orange*
*⌐ablespoon orange flower water or rose*
  *water*
*⌐z (55g) nuts, finely chopped*
*⌐easpoons cinnamon powder*
*⌐z (30g) flaked almonds, toasted*

*Method*

1. Put the couscous in a bowl and stir in the hot water, leaving to stand for 10 minutes.
2. Drain and put in a sieve or colander over boiling water and steam for about 35 minutes, or until cooked.
3. Meanwhile, soak the fruit in the orange juice and flower water.
4. Add the soaked fruit, nuts and cinnamon to the cooked couscous and press into a dish. Cool and chill.
5. Serve, turned out with flaked almonds sprinkled over the top.

# APPENDIX

## alorific Values for a Selection of Foods

*: The calorific values are for raw, whole fruit and vegetables unless otherwise stated.*

| Food | Amount | Calories (approx.) |
|---|---|---|
| almonds, shelled | 1 oz (30g) | 140 |
| apples: | | |
|    eating | 1 lb (455g) | 160 |
|    cooking | 1 lb (455g) | 140 |
|    dried | 1 oz (30g) | 75 |
|    apple juice, unsweetened | ¼ pt (140ml) | 70 |
| apricots: | | |
|    fresh | 1 lb (455g) | 115 |
|    canned in natural juice | 10 oz (285g) can | 135 |
|    dried | 1 oz (30g) | 50 |
| artichokes: | | |
|    globe | 1 lb (455g) | 130 |
|    Jerusalem | 1 lb (455g) | 200 max |
| aubergine | 1 lb (455g) | 50 |
| asparagus | 1 lb (455g) | 60 |
| avocado pear | 8 oz (225g) | 360 |
| bamboo shoots, canned | 10 oz (285g) can | 80 |
| banana, peeled | 1 oz (30g) | 25 |
| barley, pot raw | 1 oz (30g) | 85 |
| beans: | | |
|    broad, fresh or frozen | 1 oz (30g) | 15 |
|    butter, canned | 15 oz (425g) can | 280 |
|          dried | 1 oz (30g) | 70 |

| Food | Amount | Calories (approx.) |
|---|---|---|
| haricot, canned | 15 oz (425g) can | 280 |
| dried | 1 oz (30g) | 70 |
| mung, dried | 1 oz (30g) | 60 |
| pinto, dried | 1 oz (30g) | 70 |
| red kidney, canned | 15 oz (425g) | 280 |
| dried | 1 oz (30g) | 75 |
| runner, fresh or frozen | 1 oz (30g) | 5 |
| shoots or sprouts | 1 lb (455g) | 50 |
| soya, canned | 15 oz (425g) can | 500 |
| dried | 1 oz (30g) | 100 |
| beetroot, fresh, cooked | 1 oz (30g) | 15 |
| blackberries, fresh or frozen | 1 lb (455g) | 120 |
| blackcurrants, fresh or frozen | 1 lb (455g) | 120 |
| bran, natural | 1 oz (30g) | 30 |
| brazilnuts, shelled | 1 oz (30g) | 160 |
| bread, wholemeal | 1 oz (30g) | 60 |
| broccoli | 1 lb (455g) | 70 |
| Brussels sprouts | 1 lb (455g) | 80 |
| buckwheat, raw | 1 oz (30g) | 85 |
| flour | 1 oz (30g) | 100 |
| cabbage | 1 lb (455g) | 70-100 |
| carob powder | 1 oz (30g) | 80-100 |
| carrots | 1 lb (455g) | 100 |
| cashew nuts | 1 oz (30g) | 140 |
| cauliflower, trimmed | 1 lb (455g) | 40 |
| celeriac | 1 lb (455g) | 100 |
| celery | 1 head | 30 |
| cereal flakes mixed (muesli base) | 1 oz (30g) | 80-100 |
| cheese: | | |
| Cheddar or Cheshire | 1 oz (30g) | 100-120 |
| cottage | 1 oz (30g) | 25 |
| curd | 1 oz (30g) | 40 |
| Edam | 1 oz (30g) | 75 |
| Gouda | 1 oz (30g) | 75 |
| quark or skimmed milk cheese | 1 oz (30g) | 25 |
| cherries | 1 lb (455g) | 160 |
| chestnuts, fresh, skinned | 1 oz (30g) | 45 |
| dried | 1 oz (30g) | 105 |
| chick peas, canned | 15 oz (425g) can | 280 |
| dried | 1 oz (30g) | 80 |

| Food | Amount | Calories (approx.) |
|---|---|---|
| chicory | 1 lb (455g) | 40 |
| coconut: | | |
|   cream | 1 oz (30g) | 160 |
|   dessicated | 1 oz (30g) | 170 |
|   fresh | 1 oz (30g) | 90 |
| corn (maize) meal | 1 oz (30g) | 90 |
| corn on the cob | 1 lb (455g) | 380 |
| courgette | 1 lb (455g) | 100 |
| cranberries | 1 lb (455g) | 70 |
| cucumber | 1 large | 30 |
| currants | 1 oz (30g) | 60 |
| damsons | 1 lb (455g) | 150 |
| dates: | | |
|   dried, stoned | 1 oz (30g) | 70 |
|   fresh, whole | 2 medium | 40 |
| egg: | | |
|   1 whole | size 3 | 80 |
|   1 white | size 3 | 10 |
|   1 yolk | size 3 | 70 |
| fennel | 1 lb (455g) | 120 |
| figs, dried | 1 | 40 |
|   fresh | 1 | 40 |
| flour: | | |
|   wholemeal | 1 lb (455g) | 1440 |
|   soya, low fat | 1 lb (455g) | 1590 |
|      full fat | 1 lb (455g) | 1940 |
|   brown rice | 1 lb (455g) | 1620 |
| fructose | 1 oz (30g) | 100 |
| fruit salad, canned in natural juice | 10 oz (285g) can | 135 |
| gooseberries, fresh or frozen | 1 lb (455g) | 75 |
| grapefruit, canned in natural juice | 10 oz (285g) can | 120 |
|   fresh | 1 medium | 20 |
|   juice, unsweetened | ¼ pint (140ml) | 60 |
| grapes | 1 oz (30g) | 15 |
|   juice, unsweetened | ¼ pint (140ml) | 90 |
| greengages | 1 lb (455g) | 200 |
| hazelnuts, shelled | 1 oz (30g) | 110 |
| honey | 1 oz (30g) | 75 |
| kiwi fruit | 1 oz (30g) | 45 |
| ladies fingers (okra) | 1 lb (455g) | 70 |

| Food | Amount | Calories (approx.) |
|---|---|---|
| leeks | 1 lb (455g) | 50 |
| lentils, dried | 1 oz (30g) | 85 |
| macaroni, wholewheat, raw | 1 oz (30g) | 95 |
| malt extract | 1 oz (30g) | 105 |
| mandarins, canned in natural juice | 10 oz (285g) can | 80 |
|   fresh | 2 average | 40 |
| mango, fresh | 1 large | 120 |
| margarine, low fat | 1 oz (30g) | 95 |
|   vegetable | 1 oz (30g) | 200 |
| marrow | 1 lb (455g) | 40 |
| melon, honeydew | 1 lb (455g) | 60 |
|   water | 1 lb (455g) | 50 |
| milk, skimmed, fresh | 1 pint (570ml) | 180 |
|   skimmed, dried powder | 1 oz (30g) | 90 |
| millet | 1 oz (30g) | 95 |
| miso | 1 tablespoon (15ml) | 10 |
| mixed vegetables, frozen | 1 oz (30g) | 20 |
| mushrooms | 1 lb (455g) | 70 |
| nectarines | 1 lb (455g) | 200 |
| nuts, mixed | 1 oz (30g) | 140 |
| oats, regular or porridge | 1 oz (30g) | 110 |
|   jumbo | 1 oz (30g) | 110 |
| oil, vegetable | 1 tablespoon (15ml) | 135 |
| olives, stoned | 1 oz (30g) | 25 |
| onions | 1 lb (455g) | 100 |
|   spring | 1 bunch | 30 |
| orange | 1 large | 40 |
|   juice, unsweetened | ¼ pint (140ml) | 60 |
| parsley | 1 bunch | 10 |
| parsnips | 1 lb (455g) | 160 |
| passion fruit | 1 lb (455g) | 65 |
| pasta, wholewheat, raw | 1 lb (455g) | 1490 |
| peaches: | | |
|   canned in natural juice | 10 oz (285g) can | 110 |
|   fresh | 1 large | 40 |
|   dried | 1 large | 40 |
| peanuts, plain, shelled | 1 oz (30g) | 150 |
| peanut butter, natural | 1 oz (30g) | 160 |
| pears: | | |
|   canned in natural juice | 8 oz (225g) can | 100 |

| Food | Amount | Calories (approx.) |
|---|---|---|
| fresh | 1 large | 40 |
| dried | 1 large | 40 |
| peas, fresh or frozen, cooked | 1 lb (455g) | 180 |
| split, dried | 1 oz (30g) | 80 |
| peppers | 1 lb (455g) | 60 |
| pigeon peas, dried | 1 oz (30g) | 75 |
| pineapple, canned in natural juice | 8 oz (225g) can | 130 |
| fresh, whole | 1 lb (455g) | 110 |
| juice, unsweetened | ¼ pint (140ml) | 75 |
| pine kernels | 1 oz (30g) | 160 |
| pistachio nuts, shelled, raw | 1 oz (30g) | 150 |
| pitta bread, wholewheat | 1 average | 220 |
| plums, fresh, whole | 1 lb (455g) | 160 |
| potatoes | 1 lb (455g) | 340 |
| prunes, dried, whole | 1 oz (30g) | 40 |
| pumpkin | 1 lb (455g) | 55 |
| radishes | 1 lb (455g) | 30 |
| raisins | 1 oz (30g) | 60 |
| raspberries, fresh or frozen | 1 lb (455g) | 120 |
| rhubarb, fresh, raw, prepared | 1 lb (455g) | 30 |
| rice, brown, raw | 1 oz (30g) | 100 |
| flakes, raw | 1 oz (30g) | 100 |
| rum | 1 fl oz (25ml) | 65 |
| satsumas | 2 average | 40 |
| semolina, wholewheat | 1 oz (30g) | 100 |
| seeds, sesame | 1 oz (30g) | 160 |
| sunflower | 1 oz (30g) | 160 |
| sherry, dry | 1 fl oz (25ml) | 30 |
| soya milk, unsweetened | 1 pint (570ml) | 100 |
| soya sauce | 1 tablespoon (15ml) | 10 |
| strawberries, fresh or frozen | 1 lb (455g) | 115 |
| sultanas | 1 oz (30g) | 60 |
| sweet corn, canned | 12 oz (340g) can | 280 |
| fresh or frozen, cooked | 1 oz (30g) | 20 |
| spinach | 1 lb (455g) | 100 |
| spring greens | 1 lb (455g) | 20 |
| swede | 1 lb (455g) | 80 |
| sweet potatoes | 1 lb (455g) | 360 |
| tahini (sesame paste) | 1 oz (30g) | 140 |
| tangerines | 2 average | 40 |

# Simply Slim

| Food | Amount | Calories (approx.) |
|---|---|---|
| tofu | 1 oz (30g) | 15 |
| tomatoes: | | |
| canned | 14 oz (395g) can | 50 |
| fresh | 1 lb (455g) | 60 |
| juice | ¼ pint (140ml) | 25 |
| purée | 1 oz (30g) | 20 |
| turnips | 1 lb (455g) | 75 |
| walnuts | 1 oz (30g) | 130 |
| watercress | 1 bunch | 20 |
| wheatgerm | 1 oz (30g) | 60 |
| whisky | 1 fl oz (25ml) | 65 |
| wholewheat grains | 1 oz (30g) | 85 |
| wine, red, dry | 1 fl oz (25ml) | 20 |
| white, dry | 1 fl oz (25ml) | 20 |
| yeast extract | 1 teaspoon (5ml) | 10 |
| yogurt, low fat, natural | 5.3 oz (150g) | 80 |

# Calorific Values for a Selection of Snacks

| Brand | Calories |
|---|---|
| **ALLINSON** | |
| Fruit bars | |
| Banana | 90 |
| Fruit and Nut | 115 |
| Muesli | 110 |
| Wheateats | |
| Cheese flavour | 110 |
| Chilli flavour | 105 |
| Natural | 105 |
| Onion flavour | 110 |
| Peanut Butter flavour | 125 |
| Pizza flavour | 110 |
| **GRANOSE** | |
| Apricot Date bar | 85 |
| Blackberry bar | 190 |
| Cherry bar | 190 |
| Date bar | 90 |
| Date and Apricot bar | 85 |
| Date and Coconut bar | 105 |
| Date and Fig bar | 80 |
| Date and Nut bar | 95 |
| Date and Sesame bar | 95 |
| Fig and Prune bar | 80 |
| Fig and Raisin bar | 85 |
| Ginger Pear bar | 110 |
| Hazelnut bar | 240 |
| Lemon bar | 185 |
| Mixed Fruit bar | 190 |
| Orange bar | 195 |
| Strawberry bar | 190 |
| **HOLLY MILL** | |
| Apple and Hazelnut bar | 150 |
| Apricot and Almond bar | 140 |
| Banana Fruit bar | 95 |
| Banana Munch bar | 145 |
| Cereal and Nut Crunchy bar | 120 |
| Fibretime Snack bar | 150 |
| Fruit and Nut Slice | 175 |

| Brand | Calories |
|---|---|
| No Added Sugar Range bars | |
| Apple and Cardamom bar | 170 |
| Apricot and Almond bar | 160 |
| Slymbar per meal 2 bars | 230 |
| Tangy Citrus Bar | 145 |
| **JORDANS** | |
| Original Crunchy bar | |
| with Apple and Bran | 135 |
| with Coconut and Honey | 140 |
| with Honey and Almonds | 135 |
| **KP** | |
| Lower Fat Crisps | |
| all flavours | 120 |
| **LYME REGIS FOODS** | |
| Grizzly bars | |
| Apricot and Honey | 110 |
| Fruit and Honey | 110 |
| Muesli and Honey | 115 |
| **PEAK FREANS** | |
| Twiglets | |
| 25g packet | 100 |
| **PREWETT'S** | |
| Apple and Date bar | 110 |
| Apple and Ginger bar | 140 |
| Banana bar | 105 |
| Date and Fig bar | 125 |
| Fruit and Bran bar | 125 |
| Fruit and Nut bar | 135 |
| Muesli Fruit bar | 130 |
| Orange and Sultana bar | 145 |
| Savoury Hungarian Mix | 165 |
| Spicy Mexican Mix | 160 |
| Tasty Italian Mix | 165 |
| **SHEPHERDBOY FRUIT BARS** | |
| Apple Fruit and Nut bar | 140 |
| Banana Fruit and Nut bar | 165 |

| Brand | Calories |
|---|---|
| Bran Fruit and Nut bar | 125 |
| Carob Fruit and Nut bar | 165 |
| Coconut/Pineapple Fruit and Nut bar | 170 |
| Ginger Fruit and Nut bar | 165 |
| Multi Fruit bar | 90 |
| Sunflower Fruit and Nut bar | 205 |
| Tangy Fruit and Nut Bar | 135 |
| SUNWHEEL FOODS | |
| Kalibu No Added Sugar Carob bars | |

| Brand | Calories |
|---|---|
| Fruit and Nut | 290 |
| Krunchy Bran 'n' Raisin | 260 |
| Peanut | 305 |
| Peppermint | 295 |
| Plain or Orange | 295 |
| Kalibu No Added Sugar Yogurt Coated Snacks bars | |
| Banana | 100 |
| Yogurt Break bars | |
| All flavours | 315 |

# INDEX

# Simply Slim